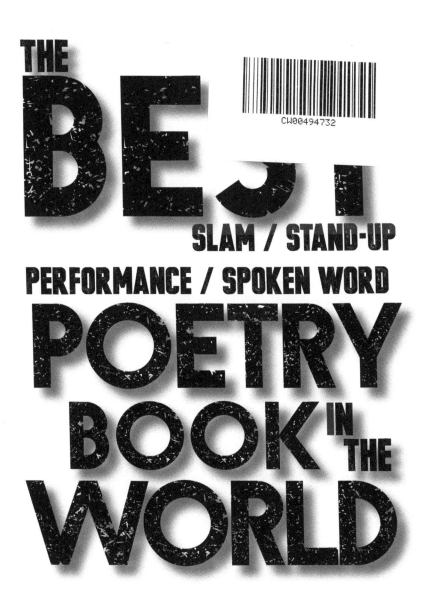

THE BEST

SLAM / STAND-UP
PERFORMANCE / SPOKEN WORD

POETRY BOOK IN THE WORLD

Edited by Jenn Hart & Clive Birnie

Burning Eye

BurningEyeBooks
Never Knowingly
Mainstream

This edition published by Burning Eye Books 2017

www.burningeye.co.uk
@burningeyebooks

Burning Eye Books
15 West Hill, Portishead, BS20 6LG

ISBN 978-1-911570-15-8

Never Knowingly
Mainstream

for Liu Xiaobo, in rememberance and solidarity

CONTENTS

START HERE – AN INTRODUCTION OF SORTS

The Best Poetry Book in the World? Maybe. The Best Slam-Stand-Up-Performance-Spoken-Word Poetry Book in the World? Why not. How many others are there? This is the point of Burning Eye. We focus on the kind of poetry that is created with the stage and live performance in mind. Our tongue in cheek title is in part a nod to the lack of consensus about the terminology applied to this genre, this movement. Movement? Yep. This is a movement. A large block of artists working within a coherent scene with a number of unifying characteristics. This is poetry written to communicate and be understood in the moment. Close reading, detailed consideration and debate about the text is not the point. This is poetry that has something to say and wants you to stop, listen and understand right now. This is poetry written in plain English. Form is not a big consideration; structure is less important than entertainment. Comedy is acceptable and often essential.

Some of these poets might refer to themselves as Spoken Word Artists rather than poets. Usually to ensure that people who think they don't like poetry can be lured into the room with the promise of something more entertaining. As Chris Redmond remarked from the Roundhouse stage last May during one of his *Tongue Fu* nights "We used to call it poetry and jazz and we played to ten people in a pub. Now we call it spoken word and improvised music and we are selling out the Roundhouse." The only consensus around the term Spoken Word is that it is "problematic". I'll leave you to look up the views of Tim Wells and Niall O'Sullivan on when Performance Poetry became Spoken Word and remind you that Spoken Word is used to cover everything from two guys (usually guys) rap battling on YouTube to a gritty one person drama performed in a respectable theatre.

Whatever you want to call it, we are its cheerleaders. It is not that there are no other publishers who will publish Slam-Stand-Up-Performance-Spoken-Word Poetry it is simply that no one else focuses on it as we do. We publish poets from all ends and angles of the movement, the slammers, the comedians, the muddy booted Glastonbury regulars, the stalwarts who slog out 25 nights at the Edinburgh Fringe every August. Poets from Devon to Scotland. Cardiff to Norwich. Poets of varied ethnicities and histories; poets of any gender, any sexuality. Poets of different religions – including Jedi. If you detect a tilt to west of centre it is because Burning Eye is run from a boxroom near Bristol.

The book is sequenced as a playlist. We encourage you to read from front to back but if you dip in and out you will find the poems are lined up in loose thematic blocks. This book will give you a sense of what Burning Eye and the first distinctive poetry movement of the 21st Century are about.

Jenn Hart & Clive Birnie, September 2017

ASH DICKINSON
SLINKY ESPADRILLES

Refluently written and inclusion, light and poignant
Jabulani D. Dramatic Verse

Sally Jenkinson

Sweat-borne Secrets

"Sally's poems are like throwglow for the soul"
Molly Blackwell, The Lovely Eggs

The Sustainable Nihilist's HANDBOOK

words by
Jonny Fluffypunk

RHYMING THUNDER
THE ALTERNATIVE BOOK OF YOUNG POETS

EDITED BY JAMES BUNTING & JACK DEAN

Mairi Campbell-Jack

This
Is
A
Poem

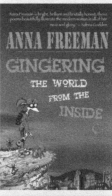

ANNA FREEMAN
GINGERING
THE WORLD
FROM THE
INSIDE

Anna Freeman is bright, brilliant and brutally honest, these poems beautifully illustrate the modern woman in all of her mess and glory. — Salena Godden

LUCY LEPCHANI
Ladygardens

Passionate and playful, angry and amused, wistful and wayward.
Ladygardens showcases Lucy's love of life and language.
- Matt Harvey

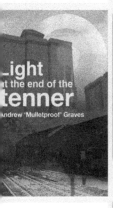

Light
at the end of the
tenner

Andrew 'Mulletproof' Graves

IN HEAVEN
THE ONIONS
MAKE YOU
LAUGH

ROB AUTON

Monkey Poet
Portrait of the Artist as a Young Simian

Poetry that hugs while it tugs, teaches while it reaches. Buy this peach then buy copies for all your friends.'
Mercun Moore

THOMMIE GILLOW

MY STEPMOTHER TRIED TO KILL ME

Thommie Gillow, The Chick-lit poet
Brandon Joe Paul Poet

ADVANCED MAGIC
FOR BEGINNERS

JOE
HAKIM

TEN THOUSAND THINGS

JEREMY TOOMBS

JACK DEAN

POEMS FOR GROWN UP CHILDREN

ALTERNATIVE
BEACH SPORTS

MICHELLE MADDEN

DAN COCKRILL
THE BOY WHO DANCED WITH TANKS

You will not pass this way
You will not pass my Paso Doble
Dance with me
With gentle cannon fodder footsteps

A caterpillar Conga
Morris the military men
Foxtrot tank track tyre
Tap to the rhythm of machine gun fire

An ironclad Flamenco
A fighting Fandango
Rumba as they rumble
To the Beijing Bolshevik Bop
Bring the killing machines to a stop

Trapeze the turret
Hold bulletproof metal tightly in my soft silent human arms
Look hard down my gun barrel stare
It's the Last Tango in Tiananmen Square

Do the Cha Cha China
It's Strictly Commie Dancing

The Judges' scores
Vladimir Lenin Goodman
"Seven"
left right left right left right left…

RAYMOND ANTROBUS
ONE NIGHT AT ZULU BAR IN CAPE TOWN

I'm dancing,
  I'm dancing more
    I'm dancing more than I ever danced.
More than I danced at my cousin's wedding,
more than I danced on my 21st Birthday
(which was a 70's roller disco)
I drink Milk Stout beer
  at the Zulu Bar
and dance with girls I won't take home.

I haven't slept in weeks,
but I'm still doing the shuffle with the 3am crowd.
It doesn't matter how much I miss my sister
even though we've never danced in the same room.
Doesn't matter that my dad won't be alive by the time
  I understand him.
Doesn't matter that I might be talking to Grandma's gravestone
by the time I'm home.
Doesn't matter that my entire family think I'm strange
and I think they are normal.
Doesn't matter that I should have told Sophie the truth
that I didn't want another person in my life that I could lose
  or let down.

Doesn't matter that it's 4am now
and behind me a girl is yelling
This music is so good it hurts!

and I'm dancing, dancing
like dancing is a kind of pain
and all I can do is
  shake.

JACK DEAN
LET THERE BE BLUD

Let there be light.
Let there be paper lanterns fluttering across motorways
for you to navigate to unseen places by.
Let there be mobile phone screens waving
like handheld stars outside clubs.
Let the insomniac tide of storefront radiance
flow sweeping over backend britons.
Let the hipster angels stay flapping into the dawn,
heads taped to speakers, solemn in prayers to synth lines.
Let us gather in messy living rooms and
drink improbable homemade cocktails and
watch rubbish movies and pause it and
say: "this bit, this bit right here,
this is a total lolocaust bruv.".
Let us stop poking and innuendo-ing and prevaricating about gender
and just have sex,
lots of mad, sweaty nutritious sex,
until it stops being such a fucking hang up for everyone.
Let the tendons of buildings echo back understanding
until we can finally make cities inhabitable,
until babies run Cribbs Causeway,
until matadors parade the bullring
and churches bleed gypsy jazz from pulpits.
Let the Five AM Maniacs bring their stubble and stimulants outside
and take in the vast, pointless, stupid gorgeousness of it all,
feel how every breeze is a poem,
how every headlight is a sonata,
so you don't always have to worry about
tacking meaning on to things like
tying waistcoats to snow leopards.
We have been tagged by the teleology police since day one,
but it's our century to fuck up,
so let us throw those anklets to the milky way
and dance like socially awkward, caucasian pieces of meteor.
Let there be knowledge and wisdom and donuts,
before they wicked-witch us into grownups.
Let the bible of my peers be
as submerged in maybes
and drowned in don't knows
as this flip-flopping age of jesters deserves.
There may be trouble ahead:
fuck it, let's remix it.

ANNA FREEMAN
I BLAME THE PARENTS

My dad
is a shabby academic,
developmental psychologist.
My mum
is an ex-Maoist,
critical-realist activist.
They're amazing
for dinner conversations,
or when you want to come out as lesbian –
they are the last people you want
to buy your back-to-school wardrobe.

I am six.
All the other six-year-old girls
have a My Little Pony.
They zoom them about the playground,
even though only some of them have wings,
they brush their tails.
I have explained to my parents
that you have to have one
or you aren't in the gang
and a debate
has ensued.
On the one hand,
insidious marketing companies
want to get their fingers into me,
to turn me into a consumer
like a witch turning a prince into a toad.
They want me to confuse product with personality,
and probably live in a pond.
On the other hand,
childhood is about tribalism
and rituals of acceptance,
and even if in this instance
this takes a materialistic form,
principles shouldn't undermine the importance
of my developing a sense of belonging
amongst my peers...
I didn't know I had any peers –

I thought that was where we went
to play penny arcade machines in Weston-Super-Mare.
It doesn't matter;
the thing about this debate is,
I'm winning.
I tell everyone at school,
I'm getting a My Little Pony today!
And they say, Which one, which one?
Is it Bowtie, is it Candyfloss?
It is neither.
The box says,
My Unicorn Friend.
It doesn't have any stars or flowers on its bum.
It is stuck
in the sitting position.
This isn't a proper one, I tell my mother.
She says,
Anna, branding is a capitalist construct.
I explain this to the other six year olds,
but they zoom away.

It is raining.
The playground is full of neat mummies,
waiting to collect neat children
under polka dot umbrellas.
Some of the mummies
have transparent plastic rain hoods that tie under the chin.
My mum has a carrier bag on her head.
She is pleased with herself for thinking of it.
She is waving at me.

It is lunch time.
What is that?
pointing at my sandwich.
Bits fall off the homemade bread when you pick it up,
it's some kind of vegan pâté the same colour as the bread.
Beside this I have a juice box,
with a prominent, unpeel-off-able reduced-price sticker,
a handful of raisins
(wrapped in Clingfilm that's been recycled so many times
it's turned into an opaque milky white ball of plastic
and skin flakes)
and natural yogurt,
spooned from the big tub into a margarine tub,
so that,

Have you got margarine for lunch?
I have to admit that, no,
I have unpackaged natural yogurt,
which is probably worse.
Between the sandwich and the raisins
a note from my mum,
hoping that I'm having a nice day.
It's a deep and confusing ache,
being ashamed of someone
who puts a heart around your name.

On my first day at big school,
we had to have black shoes and a red tie.
I had brown shoes
so my mum painted them with shoe paint,
which unpeeled into plastic strips –
bobbing black tongues
that licked the air as I walked –
and my dad bought me a hand-knitted red tie
from a charity shop;
I had a good time trying to make friends.
When I got my first period
my mum asked me if I might like to have a party.
Hello?
I know you already think I'm weird,
but would it help if I invited you to a period party?
My mum's making a beetroot hummus.

My first act of rebellion
against my atheist, scientist, Jewish-heritage father
was to join a Christian youth group
and sing hymns about the house.
Later I'd build an extensive collection of Nikes,
bring home bags of McDonald's,
convert myself into a capitalist construct –
but I couldn't shake them from my being,
I couldn't un-know what they taught me.
If I'd really wanted to rebel,
I would have become a Tory banker,
but I'm a part-time lecturer lesbian poet –
and they're very proud
that I made something of myself.

MEGAN BEECH
WHEN I GROW UP I WANT TO BE MARY BEARD

A classy, classic, classicist,
intellectually revered.
Wickedly wonderful and wise
full to brim with life,
while explaining the way in which Caligula died,
on BBC prime time.
And I would like, like her, to shine.
The kind inclined to speak her mind,
refined and blinding.
Yet I am finding
it tough
to grow up
in a world where Twitter is littered
with abuse towards women,
where intelligent, eminent, eloquent
females are met with derision.
Because she should be able to analyse Augustus' dictums
or early AD epithets,
without having to scroll through death, bomb and rape threats.
Do not tell me this is just the internet
or a public figure deserves everything they get.
Because this isn't just about one academic, it's endemic
in this society enmeshed in sexist rhetoric.
I cannot live accepting it!
Because when I grow up I want to be Mary Beard,
to wear shiny converse and converse on conquerors
and pioneers.
A sheer delight, an igniter of young minds,
but never a victim.
Like Minerva herself, a goddess of wisdom.

EMILY HARRISON
QUINOA IS ONLY SPELT LIKE THAT TO OUT THE WORKING CLASSES

The junior doctor
doesn't need to prove anything to the dinner table.

He says it all when boasting,
                'I now have the power to section people.'
I see the child
pretending
to drop the priceless vase
with over-dramatic unstable hands.

The rich kid showing off his remote-controlled
                      whatever-it-is.

The big red 'press-me-but-you-really-shouldn't-press-me'
button.

He's one of those
filling up my wine glass without my permission,
drowning my food in gravy
when I specifically said
       just a little bit.

Someone actually laughs.

And I sit in my highchair
all oblivious smiles with food-face,
the only one who had to ask for a napkin

The fork in the right hand, the knife in the wrong hand,
stop hitting yourself.

At least if someone chokes on their food
or, God forbid, their words
we're in safe hands

I force in another profiterole.
Revenge is a dish served best to whoever prepped it.

SALLY JENKINSON
THE GAS MAN COMETH

It's a gas leak, sleepyhead,
that fever fever red face fuzz.
Holy carbon monoxide,
don't shut your eyes.
We need to let the gas man in
and look at the size of his belly.

The walls are mincing themselves like liver.
I am stuck in this nest and
they've been at my solar plexus
with the ice cream scoop again.
The gas man will be back in an hour
to take another reading.

Gas Man, Gas Man
is there going to be a quiz?
It was six point fve, then two point nine
then one point something, then zero.
Are you going to go and ring your supervisor, Gas Man?

He should check too, I'm glad to know you.
Tell me again, how many months
since you last had a cigarette?
The sad twang of your cold sweat in my nostrils
so I know you're still here.

Though my eyes won't open themselves
for fear that your high-vis will blind me.

They are fluorescent gods;
we took them cups of tea at midnight.
They are not luminescent,
but they are excellent conductors of light.

The gas man says it's going to snow tonight.
He can feel it in his pipes.

KIRSTEN LUCKINS
THE STAR FERRY ROLLS ITS HIPS

Janey plays the fourth floor tiles like mahjong.
In her skyscraper, ballbreaker heels –
Click clack. Clickety clack. Hup! Jump the junkie!
The sweatshops, forty-watt, go sailing by,
Where the needles rub their cricket thighs
Up and down, up and down, all night long
Janey is a U-Boat in the seaways of Hong Kong.

Thock, thock, dock to dock,
The Star Ferry rolls its hips,
Birthing passengers like lotus pips,
Ten thousand things and all of them plastic.

All the men that Janey knows are tankers,
They hit on her and spill their loads,
Check their reflection in her periscope,
Individualities cut off at the neck-tie.
All the boys that Janey wants
Are built on dragon lines.
Like sheaths holding knives,
Their Levis hold their hip-bones,
Check out their triad tatts and mobile phones,
They love her leave her love her leave her love her leave her
love her leave her
Fall for them hard, don't even charge, blame it on 'yellow
fever'.

Thock, thock, dock to dock,
The Star Ferry rolls its hips,
Birthing passengers like lotus pips,
Ten thousand things and all of them plastic.

Forty days and forty nights of Janey,
And she's said yes to the Devil more times than three,
A sin to sell it, stupidity to give it free,
What's a girl to do?
When she wakes up it's the afternoon, and she's
Shrunk down to the size of a flea
Strung out down the rabbit hole and j-j-jittery
On cheap-speed-jackhammer-construction-jazz
It's all money no god, all colour no contrast

More is more is more is more is more
From the Peak to the shore, Lantau to Lan Kwai Fong
Gotta get out of Hong Kong.

Thock, thock, dock to dock,
The Star Ferry rolls its hips,
Birthing passengers like lotus pips,
Ten thousand things and all of them plastic.

KEITH JARRETT
A GAY POEM

They asked me if I had a gay poem
and I said, *straight up, no*
my poems don't deviate between straight lines
my poems don't *mince* their words
or bend, or make *queer* little observations

I mean, even presenting this question
puts me in a precarious position
and how would I broach the subject
with my own creation?

Like: *Excuse me – poem – are you gay?*
Have you grown up contrarily
to what I wanted you to say?
I mean, I certainly didn't write you that way –
maybe I should have peppered your verses
with sport, girls and beer
maybe I failed you –
or did another writer turn you queer?

Let's say, hypothetically, this poem is gay
maybe it's a confused poem
that just needs straightening out

maybe I could insert verses from Leviticus
speak over it in tongues, douse it in holy
water or give it a beat, beat, beat:
Batty poem fi dead! / Batty poem fi dead!
Rip up chi chi poem inna shred!

They asked me if I had a gay poem
but the truth is, I didn't know
until one of my own poems spoke up
and tapped me on the shoulder:

Look here, dad/author, I'm not confused
not alternative – and the words I choose
to marry with make me different
but not any less eloquent

26

the more your hatred tries to erase
the more your synonyms demean
the more you say you hate
the sinner and despise the sin

the more you try to clip my words
and stifle my expression
the more I know it's you, not me
who should be called into question.

PAULA VARJACK
DEAR STRAIGHT GIRL

Wait, let me specify,
because I wouldn't want to generalise unfairly.
Dear straight girl that I met
at the Gaiser party
Sunday night at Fabric
on the first of March –
well, technically the second –
sometime between 3 am and 4.

What happened?
Did you suddenly come down from
the drugs you had taken?
Or just feel differently
with your friends at your side?
OK. Rewind.

Before you'd entered my thoughts
I was just hanging out in the DJ box
watching over the dance floor,
this sea of fist pumping,
camera flashing, light strobing,
minimal techno mayhem.

I was hanging out with my mates, the DJs
Jacob and Cormac and Peter and his girl Sonoya.
I didn't know you were out there yet.
I couldn't care less that you existed.
I was in the middle of this
exclusive private party
elevated above the masses.

Dear straight girl,
later I left the DJ box,
lost myself in this ocean of ravers
when that bass line dropped
and with that bump of K
and the dab of MDMA
and the Jäger and the whiskey
and the Red Bull coursing through my veins.

My eyes clocked you, first once
then twice
until, caught up in that eye contact game,
my eyes dilated and took in all six feet
of that page three girl frame
in glorious chemically enhanced technicolour.

Dear straight girl,
you're not even my type!
OK... well, you're kind of the kind of girl
that's anyone's type,
what with the legs that never ended
embraced in black spandex
and the corseted C-cup breasts
barely covered up by your
'ironic' rock band top.
Yes, you caught my attention
but I feel I must mention
that you kissed me first!
You told me that I was 'hot'
and I... I... well...
I was too mashed
to articulate much

but I did manage to tell you
that you looked really good
against the wall I had you pinned to.
But I was fine with just dancing.
It was you! you! you!
who guided my hands
to an access-all-areas pass
to go wherever they wanted
(which was everywhere).

Dear straight girl,
you were far from complaining.
Dear straight girl,
you were definitely reciprocating.
Dear straight girl,
when you put your hands up my dress
I immediately decided to break
my new law abolishing
one-night stands and toilet cubicle sex.
I was ready to make allowances
for you!

Dear straight girl,
what happened?
Your friends appeared
and then there was this transition.
Someone said something about leaving.
You were swiftly agreeing.
Suddenly you couldn't leave fast enough.

Dear straight girl,
I wish I didn't remember your name.
Dear straight girl,
I'm sure
you didn't commit mine to your memory.
Dear straight girl,
I hate the way you left,

instantly transforming me from
this fabulous hedonist
at this exclusive private party
to a girl on her own
in a raver ocean
not nearly close enough to home.

Dear straight girl,
you know what?
This has all been irrelevant
because we'll probably never meet again
and you will never
hear this poem.

HANNAH M. TEASDALE
LESSONS FOR LOVERS OF POETS

Can we dress this up in metaphor,
wrap silk scarves of similes around us?
Perhaps leave me hanging
in drips of ellipses – maps
of erogenous zones
tracing goose bumps
like dot-to-dot colouring books;
kids' fun for adult lovers.

Tongue pushing commas –
intermission, breath for pausing,
kisses alluring me.
Alliterate me into flick, flirting,
furious, fumbling.
Keep me guessing. Please,
please, keep my interest – question
marks around my neck. Don't
let me guess. Hold
my presence with exclamation
marks skipping from my breasts.

Underline your intention
beneath my hips.
Highlight your needs
with your lips.
Acronym your pleas
inside of me.
Pinprick pupils dilate
from full stops;
calligraphy for the open-minded.
We can scribe a future
present from all of this.

Lists of others, torn
and shredded. Destroyed
as if they never existed.
Soften me with sonnets
and I will toughen you with slang.

Slip in random half-rhymes
that roll straight off your tongue...

But don't split us in half
with semi-colons,
separate beginnings too short.
Don't leave too many pauses...

Please, please finish
your sentences
as you first intended. Don't
finger-flick quotation marks
before you speak,
and if you dive in deep,
don't let go until you know
you can correction-fluid
your way back out.

Acrostic lust in
light tongue touches
Licks
Under
Silken
Thighs.
Syllable count
your foreplay
in iambic pentameter verse.
Keep the rhythm strong
but the melody light.
Leave the paraphrasing
to someone else.
And never leave sight of
how I might end up writing
this out.

Cellotaping Rain To My Cheek

Daniel Cockrill
Tony Husband

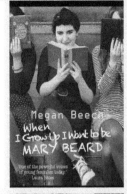

Megan Beech
When I Grow Up I Want to be MARY BEARD

'One of the powerful voices of young feminism today.'
Laura Bates

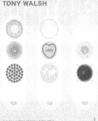

SEX & LOVE & ROCK&ROLL
TONY WALSH

BANG SAID THE GUN
AS SEEN ON TV
MUD WRESTLING WITH WORDS!
FOREWORD BY IAN McMILLAN

OPPOSITE the TOURBUS

YOU BUS

Sophia Walker

Fishing in the Aftermath
SALENA GODDEN
Poems 1994-2014

THE WOMAN WHO WAS NOT THERE

'Fearless' Benjamin Zephaniah

JOELLE TAYLOR

LUCY ENGLISH
PRAYER TO IMPERFECTION
POEMS 1996 – 2014

A.F. Harrold
Lies My Mother Never Told Me

Joyriding the Storm
Vanessa Kisuule

PETROL HONEY
ROB AUTON

The Sunshine Kid
Harry Baker

59

APPLIED MATHEMATICS
DAN SIMPSON
Burning Eye

The Secrets I Let Slip
Selina Nwulu

BOLDFACE
Nasser Hussain

POOR QUEEN
"Mab is fab" Brian Williams
PARENTAL ADVISORY EXPLICIT CONTENT
MAB JONES

JEREMY TOOMBS
MISSION BURRITO

I buy for you, my love,
a burrito
(in the end, we are
like burritos: full of beans,
wrapped together).
Another burrito I buy for me
for one isn't enough for two
and though my love
of burritos is less than my love for you,
stay away from my burrito!
That's why I bought two.

LIV TORC
NOTES FROM A SMALL ISLAND
(38 weeks pregnant and counting)

I was never really that small before
but now I'm impossible to ignore:
a space hopper slash dinosaur
waddling across the supermarket floor,
low riding an 8lb bowling ball.

Yes I'm Queen of the Oompa Loompas,
Violet Beauregard in hues of blush and sepia,
not so whiny but slightly weepier.
More than just an angry bird on a mission,
I'm a cataclysmically ferocious pufferfish,
catapult me down Frome or Totnes high street
and watch me take out small independent vintage shops
with my flailing arms and explosive posterior depth charges.

Yes, on the outside I'm taking up more and more of the room
but the territory surrounding my lungs, liver and womb
is like a slowly deflating and constrictive balloon.
You're elbowing me out of my strength and my power,
I have to psyche myself up to climb over the bath
and into the shower.

I can't sleep on my front, my back, or my right side,
my dreams are like a surreal Pink Floyd anxiety ride.
I have really clear skin
and plush shiny hair,
but I don't dare to sneeze
in my good underwear.

I can't tie my laces,
or bend down to pick up my shoes,
I can't shave my legs
or even look at my pubes.
I have to buy Double G parachutes
to constrain my dampening boobs.
My bathroom bin is full
of empty Anusol tubes.

Yes it's really quite lovely
to sacrifice and to share

but inside of my belly
it's internal organ warfare
as I sit in a fortress of cushions
gasping half lungfuls of air
and sift through NHS handouts
and gifts of pastel knitwear.

I am itchy and stretching,
drooling and retching,
never less sexy but never more letching
my bladder is full of a raging monsoon
but there's rarely more pee than a tiny teaspoon.
My hips are all achy and my chest feels like lead.
I can't get close to my husband
just hug with my head
and the minute I'm comfy I have to get out of the bed.

Each evening I bleed from my nose, anus and gums,
I binge nightly on Gaviscon and daily on Tums.
I am one body, four eyelids, two heads and four thumbs;
two heart beats, two vaginas and also two bums.

As fat as a pumpkin
with her own inner candle.
It's amazing when determined
what your body can handle;
coaxing and encouraging my significant girth
through the final few days
approaching the moment of birth
when my courage will be weighed
along with my baby and worth.

And I want to say truly that I really don't care
that I'll probably scream, pooh myself and perennially tear
because all that will matter is you're finally there
out in the open, alive and aware.
That I made you inside me,
from sperm and some cells
and several degrees of indignity hell,

and as long as we get through
with the stamp,
'Mother and baby are well',

that's all I'll remember
and maybe the only story I'll tell.

JOELLE TAYLOR
THE GIRL WHO WAS NOT ALLOWED TO SING

After school that day
they caught her
singing in the bathroom,
each note,
each dancing breath
a minor rebellion.

Insurgency in the suburbs.

They closed her mouth,
stapled between the loving
jaws of their fingers,
a muzzle
of warm Mondays.

Girls
should be silent,
especially
when they are speaking.

So

she climbed into the space
between walls
and sang;
she crawled under the lip
of the carpet
and sang.

She sang
beneath breath
beneath sound
and sang
in the cracks in the conversation
in the gap between people.

She sang
like other people cry

and her voice
divided the earth

and her voice
sent tremors across rippling continents
and her voice
teased oceans to rear on their hind legs
until it reached

the girl who was not allowed to dance.

And together
quietly
they changed the world.

AGNES TÖRÖK
MYTHS ABOUT RAPE

if even half the things you have been told about rape
were true
we would live in a very different world

if what you wear
could prevent rape
if you speaking to your friend as they walk home
could prevent rape
if you telling your daughter not to stay out late
could prevent rape
we would live in a very different world

but none of these things prevent rape
they are only the desperate scramblings for sense-making
the clinging to the illusion of control
the terrified hope
that it won't be us
who are raped
tonight

but I promise you
it will be someone
else

like a daily game of russian roulette
we never chose to play
but were born into

only the bullets don't go off
when we press the trigger

because we are not at greatest risk
when we are walking home at night
or when we are drinking
or when we are wearing skirts
or when we are flirting

the bullets go off when and where we should feel safest

nowhere are we as likely to be raped
as in our own beds

no one is as likely to rape us
as someone we trust
as someone we love

if individual choices could prevent rape
this might be a different story
but rape is not a question of risk or choice or morality
it is a question of society
our societies
which rape
has always been part of

pretending this is about individual victims
and not the faults of our entire systems
is failing to understand
why violence happens
violence does not happen because of victims' actions
or inactions
violence is the actions
of perpetrators
it is the result of millions of similar actions
made into silent norm
made systematic
made legitimate
made culture
made normal
over
millennia

SOPHIA WALKER
LESSONS IN INTIMACY

It is a picturesque English village of
church coffee mornings, Women's Institute
baking glories; this is the kind of place
still happily engaging in Morris dancing.
Daily Mail dreamland, iconic cream-tea
land, this is where Enid Blyton's
Famous Five spend their vacation time.
This is idyllic England.

At 10 am, all lessons in session, the secondary
school is quiet. I find myself in a classroom
with twenty-seven youth; we are talking about sex.
Which in essence means we're speaking
'bout the internet. This discussion is governed
by the porn they've uncovered; 'lovers'
is a meaningless word in the world of
one cup and two girls. Hold firm…
There's an unmeant pun in those words,
not handjobs but the job at hand: stand
fast against the disheartening, this
desire to protect these pubescent kids
with no concept of what consensual is.

I ask them to define intimacy.
A girl of thirteen says 'anal sex'
and every classmember agrees.
'You see, you'd only have anal sex
with a boyfriend, but you'd give
a blowjob to anyone.'

This from kids too young to have
seen Jackanory. In a village of
church coffee mornings,

Women's Institute baking glories –
while grandmas make cream cakes
pre-teens brag how cream tastes,
trading glorious hot buttered rolls
for hot footage from glory holes.
      This is
where innocence and the internet
intersect: the exact point
kids begin thinking
intimacy means anal sex.

THOMMIE GILLOW
SASHA

If I eat three Weight Watchers Mars bars
does that count as a binge session?
and when David comes home from
not quite working and complains because
I hung his saggy elastic boxer-shorts up
outside the flat where our only neighbour
could see them but the air could make them
smell so fresh do I ask him about the
cauliflower and garlic he forgot to buy?
Do I moan that I am the fabric of this sari
we are woven up in and yet I have lost
my beginnings, and my end? Should I?

I open the fridge and see that the C.I.A.
bugged my parmesan due to the fact
it has been so long sitting there it is not at risk
of escape. I knew there was a buzzing
on my phone line but thought it was the flies
around the nappies David refuses to touch.
He says the korma stains deter him and he
has such sensitive skin. The baby doesn't
cry anymore, not since prohibition and
that man who masturbates in our cellar.
I pinched him the other day to check
that he was real and he laughed.

David likes to watch the television and calls
the remote Suzie, like a girlfriend
he had in school. She let him shag her places I have
never let him near and I don't mean Bracknell.
I spend my evening finding alternative places
to hang the baby grows and wonder if
my ears might be a good solution, and my
coat-hanger nipples. I used to jingle if
you shook me out and my gold threads catch the light,
yet now my step hardly breaks the flow
of the Daily Show, or the slapping from the basement.
If I eat three Weight Watchers Mars bars
does that make me a binge eater? Does it make
me real? If I eat three Weight Watchers
Mars bars will it help me breathe?

ROSY CARRICK
VANISHING ACT

The hunger is the proof I can do it.
I scrabble the bony bits all of the time,
evicting the meat of my body.
I press my ankles and knees together
and stand
with a lit lamp behind me
fully naked in front of the mirror
then use my hands to cup up and squeeze back tight
the top of each anxious thigh.
The possibility of all this extra light
from between my legs
makes excitement beat in my gut
and steadies my aim.
I photo my torso from every angle
in each degree of shadow;
edifying ribs
and stroking clean the breastbone.
All of a sudden I've been at it close to a day,
every night is the same
though it's only the best when it's clear that I'm shrinking in earnest
and then I am lost.
The lameness of fat – I get it
around my hips,
heavy as horse collar,
it needles the truth:
I'm a greedy girl.
Unphysical.
I eat beyond the point of sustenance.
Sometimes I think my aim is to be muscular;
easily run ten miles or climb a rope like children do
but knowing the magic of growing smaller
remains the unspeakable truth.
Ideally,
I would scrape around;
an optical illusion or a skeleton in skin
with just,
I guess,
sufficient muscle left to reach a destination.

TINA SELDERHOLM
CONSIDER THE CUPCAKE

Consider its curves,
its whips, its whirls,
consider the glint
of its frosting.
The way it tickles
your fancy, whispering,
Lick me.

Consider you promised
not to eat them again,
but the ache in your gut
insists you're hungry
for something.
And it's just
an ickle cupcake,
whispering,
Lick me, lick me.

And the hollow grows
with every glance,
your conscience and desire
in an intricate dance,
because you're hungry
for something,
and the more you say *No,*
the more you want to;
the more you say *Don't,*
the more it shouts *Do!*
You're hungry
for something,
for God's sake,
lick me, lick me, lick me.

So strip off the casing,
heart racing at each rip.
Dip your finger in the icing,
let your teeth penetrate.

Close your eyes,
dream of parties
back when life was fun,
as its sweetness disperses
on your impatient tongue.

So you've licked.
Deed done.
Your stomach seems full,
but your mind screams, *More!*
And as you've broken
your promise anyway…

Stick another in your mouth
even faster than the last.
No time to feel queasy,
no chance to grasp
that you're starving
for something
much larger than cake.
Plugging the gap
with carbohydrates,
seduced by the wiles
of sugar and glaze,
caught in a spiral

you thought was escape.

CRYSSE MORRISON
BUNGEE JUMPING CRUMBLIES

Look at them! It's obscene.
Wrinklies, tottering round Topshop!
They should act their age, not their fuck-me shoe size –
should be saving their pension, not prancing at parties
wanton and plastered, still trance-dancing,
still backpacking the golden road to summer lands.

Retiring? They don't know the meaning of the word –
refusing to age gracefully, won't go quiet
into that genteel twilight good night –
collecting tattoos instead of bus passes,
puckering sundried faces for kisses,
mutton-dressed brazen lambs, perpetual Peter Pans!
What do they think they're like?

This is what I think:
I'm not a sheep to be cut and devoured.
I'm not looking for a Never-Never land.
So don't confuse me with someone who wants
to be part of those fictions – why should I
change my life-long convictions?
Curiosity. Boldness. Lust for life.

LUCY LEPCHANI
HOW TO BE DESIRABLE

Media says that you've got to get fit,
lose a lot of weight, not just a little bit,
got to get smooth skinned, got to get a tan,
got to get fixed up if you want to get a man.

Media says that you've got to stay young,
got to get your lips plumped, eyelids done,
chemical peel all wrinkles from your skin,
just a little bitty dimple and you've got to get thin.

Then media says that you've got to get thinner,
look at these celebrities, eat no dinner,
got to suck the fat from your belly and your hips,
stick it in your breasts and a bit into your lips.

Got to get big tits, silicone discs,
up a triple cup size never mind the risk,
designer vaginas, tighter than a glove,
got to fit right or you won't get loved.

Live the look and love the look – read the magazines,
be a Facebook profile picture queen,
got to get a following, got to get a plan,
got to get fixed up or you won't get a man.

Media says create illusions of success,
high-achieve with white teeth, smile to impress!
Got to get a guru, got to be beautiful,
got to look natural on all things pharmaceutical.

Media morons manipulate the facts,
say: epilate, depilate, pluck and wax!
Neaten your bikini lines, Hollywood, Brazilian!
(Itching for a fortnight, then you do it all again).

Fix it up, hitch it up, turn yourself around again!
Needles full of fillers, botox and collagen!
Gravity will bitch it up, got to fix it all again!
Turn around and lose a pound again again again AGAIN!

Get it from the clinic, get it on credit,
cosmetic medics do it Direct Debit,
Don't let yourself go (someone famous said it)
and don't let others know how much of you, you have to edit.

Media mocks with misogynist taboos.
Older, fatter women are the losers in the news.
Thinking of adventures underneath the knife?
Sisters, get a grip now. Go and get a life!

SALENA GODDEN
MY TITS ARE MORE FEMINIST THAN YOUR TITS

My tits are more feminist than your tits
My tits are more feminist than your tits
No. My tits are more feminist than your tits
No. My tits. My tits. No my tits. No my tits actually
My tits are the feminist tits
No. My tits are the feminist tits

Well, my tits are gay tits. My tits are lesbian tits
My tits are minority tits. My tits are black tits
My tits are more black than your black tits
And my tits are more feminist than your tits

My tits are trans tits. My tits identify as being women's tits
My tits have no say. My tits have no voice
My tits have no vote. My tits have no choice
My tits have got no fucking space to be tits

My tits are more feminist than your tits
My tits are more feminist than your tits
No, my tits are more feminist than your tits
The tits are fighting the tits. The tits are fighting the tits

Look at her tits. Look at those tits
Her tits are good tits
Those are some good tits
Her tits are productive tits
Her tits breast fed her babies
Her tits breast feed in public
Look at those tits
Her tits are leaking milk
Those are disgusting milky tits
Look at those tits

Look at those tits
Her tits are childless
Those tits are just for titillation
Her tits are fake plastic boob job tits
Page three, shame on her tits
Shame on those tits

Look at her tits

Look at those tits
Her tits are ageing badly
Her tits were legends
Yeah, but her tits are scientology tits now
Her tits were seen drunk in public
One tit popped out
I could see some side boob. Side boob
Did you see the side boob? Side boob?
What the fuck is side boob? Side boob?

Look at her tits
Look at those tits
Those are not real women's tits
Those tits don't do the school run
Those tits don't juggle both motherhood tits and career tits
Those are not the tits of a working mum

Look at her tits
Look at those tits
Those tits are active tits
Positive and sporty tits
Those tits are doing a marathon for cancer and tits
For cancer and tits. Let's support the tits
Do you support your tits?

My tits drank rum all night and cried
My tits can be very naughty
Don't judge my tits
Walk a mile in my bra
See how you like them tits

Look at her tits
Look at those tits
Her tits were asking for it
Her tits were begging for it
Those are the tits of a whore!
Let's slut shame those tits!

Stop. Tits. No
Sign this petition
Sign my Pet. Tit. Tion.
Sign my tits

Because my tits are more feminist than your tits
My tits are more feminist than your tits

No. My tits are more feminist than your tits
No. My tits are more feminist than yours
Bitchy tits. Bitter tits. Cunty tits
Sub tweet tits. Anti tits. Resting bitch face tits
Tits! Tits! Say it out loud: TITS

Those are my sisters tits
We are all sisters and we all have tits
Would you talk to your mothers tits like that?
Think about it. Think about tits. Think about it Think about tits
Because your daughters will have tits one day

Stop abusing the tits
Raped tits. Hurt tits
Benefit cut tits. Vulnerable tits
Her tits have no love
Her tits have no home
Her tits are refugee tits
Her tits are at war
Her tits sit in a prison camp
Her tits are immigrant tits
Drowning in the ocean tits
Tits on opposite sides of the barbed wire fence tits
Rape is a weapon of war
Domestic violence
Murdered tits. Every fucking day. Murdered tits

All tits are equal, but some tits are more equal than others
I think all women should do what the fuck they like with their own tits
To bra and not to bra is not a question
You don't have to be such a dick about tits

I wish everyone would stop being such a dick about tits

Because all we are saying is
Give tits a chance
All we are saying is
Give tits some peace
All we are saying is
Give tits a chance
All we are saying is give tits some
Peace.

JENN HART
LET LOOSE LUCY

Lucy is sixteen, sick of school politics
dictated by pretty appearances,
she wants to be different
likes listening to heavy, fast songs
about being young and reckless
and after weeks of begging her parents
she gets a suprise in the post -
two tickets to her first ever punk rock show.

She spends days selecting the right outfit
shop modded rips and ladders,
tarten school skirts and fingerless gloves,
wears leopard print and suspender belts
because nothing says 'REBEL' like a girl
showing her underwear.

On the night of the show Lucy anxiously
approaches the crowd
her heart thumping as they look her up and down
calculating those 'punk points'
and she congratulates herself on the impact her outfit has.
Inside she picks her spot, think she's in luck
in front of the barrier.
Her heroes are playing the songs
she ruined the repeat button over
screaming along,
passion pumping through her lungs until
she is winded, pinned against the fans either side of her
because men twice her size are pummeling each other
in the name of music.
She's pushing back but is slammed into place
out of the cockpit
into the wall.

So Lucy stands back with the retired,
forever on edge on the edge of a punch up
where every other runt is on the outside
trying to barge their way in

She wants to be with her friends admidst the chaos
her fist in the air.
But she can no longer ignore her injuries and

she is no longer having fun
so she slinks back in to the unmoving
pretends she content to be out of the way.

Four years later
Lucy is fingering a guitar and watching a documentary on punk.
The only representation for her gender is
Golden Debbie Harry,
Heartbreaker Brody Dalle and
Washed-up, Slut-shamed Courtney Love

She still listens to bands all about political liberation
but every now and again there's a song about
some crazy stalker woman,
they put a brass line in it so everyone is singing
about this girl's heartbreak
or maybe this girl just wanted to be friends
but they've dressed her up as a slut to
make everyone dance at her expense.

Lucy still goes to shows but stands to the side
isn't introduced because she's nobody's prize
sick of being asked which member of the band she's with.
Stops her small talk with merch guys
who don't have time for groupies.

Lucy is sick of being excluded from a scene
assumed to be inclusive
tired of fighting for her space from those who
think letting women in is an act of kindness.
She is about to give up
to stay no better than an instrument
when in that corner that she has been confind to
finds the sorts who dance without harressment
those who play music from patronising judgement
and all of them still fighting a barage of segregation.

They say

'Let loose, Lucy! Give 'em hell!
Punk rock is not about   giving up or giving in so
fuck the manarchists and their phobic shit!'

Boys, be cool for once in your lives
stand aside, the time has arrived for

          all women to the front.

SAM BOARER
REAL GROWN UP WOMEN

Real grown up women buy their make-up from make-up counters,
they don't rifle through the bargain bin at Superdrug
looking for the least used tester lipstick.

Grown up women don't accidentally grow penicillin
in their used coffee cups,
and they definitely don't tell a man who was flirting with them
that they have dandruff of the face.

Grown up women do not attempt to cut and dye their own hair
and end up looking like a cross between
a scarecrow and Boris Johnson.
They go to high end salons and are treated like a princess
by an overpaid stylist
named after the country he was conceived in.

Grown up women come out of that salon
looking like Kim Kardashian,
with a complimentary Kanye West
and a designer vagina to match.

Real Grown up women don't ask a room full of strangers
if she's the only one with a vagina acidic enough
to bleach her knickers,
or sing born free every time they
come out of the shower freshly shaved.

Talking of vaginas, grown up women get waxes,
they don't shave their own pubic hair
and walk around for a week
indiscreetly scratching themselves.

A real grown up woman has a steady boyfriend
who brings her flowers, but isn't too clingy.
She doesn't get hit on by a drunk sixty-eight year old
who accidentally walked into a poetry show
and called her a 'very sensual vixen'.

A real grown up woman doesn't
nap on a bed full of dishes

doesn't have Supernoodles for dinner
or get chewing gum stuck in her pubic hair.
She doesn't do a twenty minute poetry set
With a light shining up her skirt,
Doesn't come on her period during sex,
Doesn't stalk the fit guy who
Works in Urban Outfitters
And definitely doesn't drunkenly tell men
She'll kiss them on the penis.

But God - she must have a boring life.

Talk
you
round
till dark

REBECCA TANTONY

with illustrations by
ANNA HIGGIE

BURNING BOOKS

JESS GREEN

MARK GRIST
ROGUE TEACHER

BLITZ

Are You as
Single
as That
Cream?

Poems and Pick Ups
by
Amy McAllister

LIV TORC

CHERRY PIE
by Hollie McNish

Lydia
Towsey

The Venus
Papers

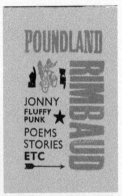

POUNDLAND
RIMBAUD

JONNY
FLUFFY
PUNK
POEMS
STORIES
ETC

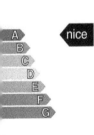

A
B
C
D
E
F
G

nice

Robert Garnham

Things
You
FIND
in a Poet's
Beard
A.F Harrold

EMILY HARRISON
I CAN'T SLEEP 'CAUSE MY BED'S
ON FIRE

Underneath the Rain
When I Remembered Everything
Molly Case

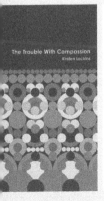

The Trouble With Compassion
Kirsten Luckins

let
the
pig
out

STRANGE KEYS
ASH DICKINSON

Poems by
Stef M.

A. F. HARROLD
THE DECREPITUDE OF THE POET

I've got athlete's foot.
I've got miner's lung.
I've got cauliflower ear
and carpenter's thumb.

I've got housemaid's knee.
I've got rising damp.
I've got writer's block
and writer's cramp.

I've got taxman's twitch.
I've got librarian's eye.
I've got poker face
and spinster's sigh.

I've got tennis elbow.
I've got sousaphone pout.
I've got trumpeter's cheek
and port-drinker's gout.

I've got golfer's grip.
I've got jogger's nipple.
I've got OAP's hip
and footballer's dribble.

I've got policeman's truncheon.
I've got burglar's stoop.
I've got wino's nose
and brewer's droop.

I've got bishop's fnger.
I've got acrobat's back.
I've got juggler's balls
and postman's sack.

HARRY BAKER
PAPER PEOPLE

I like people.
I'd like some paper people.
They'd be purple paper people.
Maybe pop-up purple paper people.
Proper pop-up purple paper people.
How do you prop up proper pop-up purple paper people?

I'd probably prop up proper pop-up purple paper people
with a proper pop-up purple people paperclip,
but I'd pre-prepare appropriate adhesives as alternatives,
a cheeky pack of Blu-Tack just in case the paper slipped.
I could build a pop-up metropolis.
But I wouldn't wanna deal with all the
paper people politics,
paper politicians with their
paper-thin policies,
broken promises
without appropriate apologies.

There'd be a little paper me.
And a little paper you.
And we'd watch paper TV,
and it would all be pay-per-view.
We'd see the poppy paper rappers
rap about their paper package,
or watch paper people carriers
get stuck in paper traffic,
on the A4.

There'd be a paper
princess Kate,
but we'd all stare at
paper Pippa.
And we'd all live in fear of
killer Jack the Paper-Ripper,
because the paper propaganda
propagates the people's prejudices,
papers printing pictures of the
photogenic terrorists.

It's a little paper me.

And a little paper you.
And in a pop-up population
people's problems pop up too.

There'd be that pompous paper parliament
who remained out of touch,
and who ignored the people's protests about
all the paper cuts,
then the peaceful paper protests
would get blown to paper pieces,
by the confetti cannons
manned by pre-emptive police.

Yes there'd still be
paper money,
so there'd still be
paper greed,
and paper piggy bankers
pocketing more than they need,
purchasing the potpourri
to pepper their paper properties,
while others live in poverty
and ain't acknowledged properly.

A proper poor economy,
where so many are proper poor,
yet while their needs get ignored,
the money goes to big wars.
Origami armies
unfold plans for paper planes,
while we remain imprisoned
by our own paper chains,
but the greater shame,
is that it always seem to
stay the same
What changes is who's in power,
choosing how to
lay the blame,
they're naming names,
forgetting these are names of people,
because in the end
it all comes down to people.

I like people.
Because even when the situation's dire,

it is only ever people
who are able to inspire,
and on paper,
it's hard to see how we all cope.
But in the bottom of Pandora's box
there's still hope,
and I still hope
because I believe in people.

People like my grandparents.
Who every single day since I was born,
have taken time out of their morning
to pray for me.
That's 8296 days straight
of someone checking I'm okay,
and that's amazing.
People like my aunt who puts on plays with prisoners.
People who are capable of genuine forgiveness.
People like the persecuted Palestinians.
People who go out of their way to make your life better,
and expect nothing in return.

People have potential
to be powerful.
Just because the people in power
tend to pretend to be victims,
we don't all need to succumb to the system.
A paper population is no different.

There's a little paper me.
And a little paper you.
And we could watch paper TV
and it would all be pay-per-view,
and in a pop-up population
people's problems pop up too,
but even if the whole world fell apart
then we'd still make it through.

Because we're people.

ROBERT GARNHAM
POEM

The moon isn't really called 'the moon'.
It's actually called Simon.
It's a secret that the astronomers
Don't want us to know
Because they think it's a bit embarrassing
That the moon is really called Simon.
It sounds more like a moustachioed gas boiler
Inspector from Kettering
Than an interplanetary body.

Moon. Simon. Simon. Moon.

1950s.
NASA.
1950s.
NASA.
Let's all ride a rocket ship
To the Simon.
Let's all ride a rocket ship
To the Simon.
Count down, six, five,
Four, three,
Two, one.
Look out, Groovy Simon,
Here we come!

A hop, a skip and a jump
On the surface of Simon.
Poking poking poking around
On the surface of Simon.
Deary me, that sounds like a porn film.
(Mind you, I'd watch it.)

Moon. Simon. Simon. Moon.

I spent a night of passion with a particle physicist,
And we danced under the stars.
And we held each other tight.
In the absolute oneness of our romance,
I asked her what she thought of the Simon.
She slapped me.

Moon. Simon. Simon. Moon.

Simon is the size of Australia,
Except it's spherical, which Australia isn't.

It's got a B-side.
It's got a B-side.
A dark side.
Simon's got a dark side.
If Australia had a dark side,
They'd probably fill it up with
More of those fiddly marsupials.

Moon. Simon. Simon. Moon.

Dave says the Milky Way is slightly moist.
Dave says Venus is shaped like a duck.
Dave says Jupiter is fluffy
And it was probed in the 1970s.
I often take heed of Dave's knowledge
Though he reckons he was
Also probed in the 1970s.
Dave's a bit weird sometimes.

Moon. Simon. Simon. Moon.

I was floating through the universe the other day
Like a dolphin in Primark.
The airless vacuum made my hair all frizzy.
As I re-entered the atmosphere
I brushed the surface of Simon.

Moon. Simon. Simon. Moon.

The moon should wear a wig.
That will jazz it up a bit.
Nothing too flash,
But something to conceal its baldness.
We'll work on its craters
Laters.

Moon. Simon. Simon. Moon.

I bound across your surface
Like an astronaut with a bus to catch.
Bouncy bouncy bouncy.
Flump flump flump.
I bound across your surface
Like a potato rolling down the stairs.
Bouncy bouncy bouncy.
Plop plop plop.

Moon. Simon. Simon. Moon.

Simon, Simon, in the night sky.
I often wonder why,
When night clouds drift by,
You throw down your lunar glow,
Throw down your lunar glow,
But to the earth it doesn't go,

Because of all those clouds
That I just mentioned.
Did you switch off the light, Moon Simon?
Click, click, off.

Moon. Simon. Simon. Moon.

The moon isn't really made of cheese.
Otherwise Apollo 11 would have brought back a sandwich.
The lunar module was called the Eagle
But its occupants nicknamed it 'Timothy'.
Neil Armstrong wasn't the first man on the moon.
It was the cameraman.
I saw a documentary about methods of attaching panels to ships.
It was riveting.

I put my name down for origami classes.
But they folded.

The surface of the moon is barren
And lacking in atmosphere.
Newton Abbot.
The moon isn't always called Simon.
On its birthday it's called Mr Plumbridge.
On its birthday it's called Mr Plumbridge.
On its birthday it's called Mr Plumbridge.
On its birthday it's called Mr Plumbridge.

Moon. Simon. Simon. Moon.

Fishy fishy sparkle sparkle,
Swim fish swim.
Fishy fishy sparkle sparkle,
The sun is also called Jim.

Moon. Simon. Simon. Moon.
Moon. Simon. Simon. Moon.
Simon. Moon. Simon.
Simon. Moon. Simon. Simon.
Moon. Simon. Simon. Moon.

MATT PANESH (MONKEY POET)
TEA

Yes. It was worth the brutality,
the Indian suppression,
for this little bag of bliss,
the Englishman's confection.

You see,
back in the early days
the East India Company
responsible for Britain's tea,
had its own army
to guarantee
the regularity
of supply.

Ah! The cup of tea.
Not only does it taste marvellously,
but you see, symbolically,
even though the contents of the cup may change,
don't think it strange,
that whether fabric, or diamonds,
or oil,
or mineral wealth won through business
or spoils...
It'll all come over like a cup of tea,
whether Chinese, African or Iraqi.
You see –
proper tea is theft.

ASH DICKINSON
GLASS COFFIN COFFEE TABLE WIFE

stiff under magazines in the afterlife
Glass Coffin Coffee Table Wife
she'd been married to a charmer
an enthusiastic embalmer
so when death claimed her/ he framed her
laid her down, took off her glasses
preserved her with gases
till death us do part
she's now a work of art
with a hot / mug / mark

inseparable in life, inseparable in death
invited round to meet the old ball and chain
lift up your chips, sonny
she's there- smiling squarely through the pane
in life, she'd cooked all his meals
now, she's been fitted with wheels
he pushes her to the supermarket
once more down the aisle
she doubles up as a shopping cart
loaded down with pies, pasties, pastries
toasties, tasties and tarts
she's surprisingly little trouble to park
this work of art
with a hot / mug / mark

February, a burglary
he awakes to find his DVD/ CD/ TV/ gone
and so is she
his taxidermy bride/ alive on the outside
her absence highlights how the sun has dyed the carpet
he doesn't report it to the police-
too inconsolable with grief
broken-hearted for his clear-departed
months later/ he/ too/ dies
at the same time in the capital
a dead woman, in a glass coffin
scoops the Turner Prize
taken in the dark, displayed as objet d'art
forever more, a work of art
with a hot/ mug/ mark

JOHNNY FLUFFYPUNK
COFFEE

You're more special than the special of Special Brew,
you're the taste of new day's dawning,
you're the dark Guatemalan hanging round my
                              breakfast-bar,
you're the bomb without a warning.
You're Domestos in my tired veins
beneath the rim of tired brain;
you flush me sane, I can't complain.
You're an army turned to liquid
& you're waging war on yawning.

You're my croissant's perfect lover.
You're my cup of electric wet.
If I drink you before I go to sleep
then sleep at once becomes a very outside bet.

Coffee: let me smell you.
Coffee: let me spell you out -
C - Come alive at your hot kiss
O - so much better than tea
F - Free cups before 9
F - Fuck Tea
E - Energy gravel
E - Essence of space travel condensed to beverage form.

You're my profound grounds,
you're my make-me-louder powder.
You're my heavenly ebony pick-up juice,
you free my voice. You fill my vowels,
you loosen up my morning bowels.
I need towels if I spill you

& you fill my loving cup
& knock off my socks
& you unlock my box
& you put oil on the dried wood of my writer's block.

Coffee: you've earned first place.
Coffee: you give me the energy to still believe in the
revolutionary potential of the human race.
Coffee: you're the ink-blood of the poet's pen
& Coffee: you gild the silver tongues of would-be-lovers...

For example:

When I was in that cafe in Llanidloes & the girl at the counter was cutting up extra thick slices of apricot flapjack before turning her back & invoking the mystic gurgle of the percolator & as I smelt the cup of hot, black, shamanic brew I turned to her and said *Oi you, yes, you! you're an angel you are; an angel with wings flecked with flapjack crumbs and fringed with cappuccino froth! Let's make love upon your pile of neatlyfolded serviettes and smear each other in the organic mayonnaise for which this establishment is so justly famous!* & she gazed down at me through a halo of condensing steam and said *you again...*

ROB AUTON
FOOTBALLER'S LIFE FOR ME

I work in an art supplies shop
I get paid £250,000 a week
Crowds of screaming fans gather at the windows of the shop
Wearing replicas of my staff T-shirt that say STAFF on the back
They cheer me on with my daily tasks through chant and song
Stack those paint pots, stack those paint pots, stack those paint
pots and sell them, stack those paint pots and sell them

If I sell a particularly expensive set of oil paints the cheers can
be heard right across Soho

Young children copy my unique method of stocktaking
masking tape and rival art shops bid to get me on their books
of watercolour paper

The injuries I suffer at work such as paper cuts from cardboard
boxes
Are dealt with on the spot by the staff physio
Are you sure that you can continue to work today Rob? Asks
the physio
Yes I can continue, I reply, to the delight of my screaming fans
at the window

TV stations fight for the rights to televise footage from the
shops CCTV cameras
So the nation can see how I collapse a cardboard box
Or inform a customer
Yes Madam, I'm sorry, these are the only colours of pencil
sharpeners that we sell

JOE HAKIM
GLASS CABINET

I knew it was coming when they
halved the till-floats. A couple of
days later, my manager called me.
Her voice faltered as she told me
the news, as though she was informing
a relative of a loved-one's passing.

They closed the store when we had
the emergency-meeting. I realised
it was the first time that I had seen
all the staff in the same room at the
same time. Someone boiled the kettle
and we had tea, coffee and biscuits.

We pulled up chairs and sat round
as she read out the email from head office.
She tried to be as professional
as possible, but you could see she
was upset. After all, she had been
working for the same company for

over 25 years. For some reason, it didn't
feel significant. It wasn't as momentous
as a pit closure or the halting of a production line
for example, despite the fact that
we were in one of the last shops in our
area. Nobody had any questions.

When the meeting was over, our
manager pinned the notice to the door,
and then she turned out the lights and
locked up the store. It was cold outside,
so I went home and waited for someone
to build another super-market somewhere.

SELINA NWULU
CURRICULUM VITAE

One summer I dreamt in French for the first time.
I backpacked, got stranded in Prague, slept by French lakes
and fell in whimsy with inappropriate boys (from afar).

Later, I would escape to a dot in the Indian Ocean.
I'd rediscover my skin in rich mahogany,
sleep on mountain tops and never see so many stars.
For a second I would taste freedom.

You travelled where?
sneers the First Suit, headbutting my thoughts.
OK, sure, fine – but what did you actually do?

Bird song memories morph into the shrill
of job centre phones. The Suit's eyebrows
nail me to the chair. The wind disappears,
caution re-finds me and sits on my shoulder,
regrets hiss at my ear –
another stagnant statistic becoming.

Weeks roll on, to-and-fro, to-and-fro.
Signed on. Switched off. Monotonous actions
in the room of tripped ambition. And I do learn
new tricks, like finding strength in my words
and learning how to make the perfect cup of
green tea during the commercial breaks of
Come Dine with Me.

Daytime re-runs, time passes and my life
becomes a klaxon, the job centre pulls
on my reins and squeezes my mind of its optimism.

So what kind of employment are you looking for?
parrots Suit Two.

I want to write. I want to save myself
and the world from its suffocating anguish.
I want to give a damn, honestly I do, because
in a world that turns in lust for
yen, dollar, sterling, I want to do something more,
something that really matters.

Do you know what I mean?

So... communications, then?

Suit Two misspells *communication*.

I sink further in my polyester seat,
look skyward but can't see the stars
anymore, just the plaster ceiling cracks.

So what exactly are you doing to look for work?
sighs Suit Three.

I'm falling in love with jobs that pay me back
in silence and automated emails.

I'm having my heart broken by rejection messages,
informing me of unsuccessful applications.

I'm trying to woo and charm recruiters but in a crowd
of desperate people I'm just another pixel in a billboard poster.

I used to think I was somebody.
But sitting in this doleful room,
I watch all of my armour,
these adventures and life philosophies,
tumble around my feet.

Till I am left, whittled down to a crisp CV
polluted with half plans and exaggerations.

I speak several languages, you know.
I can very nearly juggle with four balls.
I did a course in French sign language.
My grandmother lived till she was 108.
I once hiked a volcano.
I make a mean chickpea stew.

I don't think you care.

HOLLIE MCNISH
MATHEMATHICS

he says
those goddamn pakistanis and their goddamn corner shops
built a shop on every corner – took our british workers jobs
he says
those goddamn chinese and their goddamn china shops
i tell him they're from vietnam but he doesn't give a toss
i ask him what was there before that *damn japan man's shop?*
he stares at me and dreams a scene of british workers' jobs
of full-time full-employment before the goddamn boats all came
where everybody went to work for full-time full-hours every day
a british business stood there first – he claims – *before the bloody*
irish came
now british people lost their jobs and bloody turkish there to
blame
i ask him how he knows that fact – he says – *because it's true*
i ask him how he knows it's fact – he says – *it says it in the news*
every time a somali comes here they take a job from us
the mathematics one for one – from us to them – it just adds up
he bites his cake he sips his brew he says again he knows the plot
the goddamn caribbeans came and now good folk here don't
have jobs
i ask him what was there before the *goddamn persian curtain shop*
i show him architects' plans
empty plots and closed off land
there was no goddamn shop before those pakistanis came and
planned
man – i am sick of crappy mathematics
because i love a bit of sums
i spent three years into economics
and i geek out over calculus
and when i meet these paper claims

that one of every new that came
takes away *our* daily wage
i desperately want to scream
your maths is stuck-in primary
because some who come here also spend
and some who come here also lend
and some who come here also tend
to set up work which employs them
and all those balance sheets and trends
they work with numbers – not with men
and all this goddamn heated talk
ignores the trade the polish brought
ignores the men they give work to
not plumbing jobs but further too
ignores the guys they buy stock from
accountants builders on and on
and i know it's nice to have someone
to blame our lack of jobs upon
but immigration's not that plain
despite the sums inside our brains
as one for one
as him for you
as if he goes *home* they'll employ you
because sometimes one that comes makes two
and sometimes one can add three more
and sometimes two times two is much much more than four
and most times immigrants bring more than minuses

TOBY CAMPION
MAKE LEICESTER BRITISH

They're talking about you, Leicester.
Saying you have too much curry sauce
on your fish and chips to taste like home.
Too many colours in your Union Jack
for it to be flown full mast, saying you ain't British.
And you lot can't even get along with your own.
They are calling you a broken home.

Tell them the truth, Leicester.

Tell them how I only made Sheep #2 in our school nativity,
but was cast as Rama in the Diwali play that year
and I was bloody great. Classmates of all faiths
gathered to celebrate acceptance of light.
How you raised hungry minds,
bellies full; Tarka Daal, Jerk chicken, Shepard's pie.
School trips to churches, gurdwaras, mosques,
apart from the free food, all just buildings to us.
Tell them of the day that bus full of hate
rolled up on your doorstep,
the angry men, an organised pack;
a "league of defence" which only seemed to attack.
Yet despite the wrath of those furious men,
an entire city stood united to face them.

Tell them, Leicester.

City who says it like it is,
they're twisting your turnstiles
into a picture which doesn't exist;
bandits, beggars and the bad in between,
headline after headline, day after day.
But you are the one who stands in their way,
Leicester. Because you work.
Your cobbled streets bow at the feet
of sari shops and bakeries holding hands,
masala fireworks sizzling bright, stretching out
to kiss the dales goodnight.

Tell them.

Because they have forgotten their history.
1915. 1940s. Empire Windrush.
London Transport. NHS.
Throughout time "un-British" support
has saved us from our own mess.
Let us not twist ourselves into a picture
which does not exist,
we who says it like it is.
Immigrants helped build this country,
let fact be known.
If they are looking for someone to blame
for the new mess they are in,

Tell them

to look a little closer to home.

ANDREW GRAVES
RADFORD ROAD

A saffron dance
on a cloudless day
bounds across
a taxi bonnet,

forms a
swirling sari love,
written in a
red brick sonnet

for incense burning
Naan bread ovens
sweating, promised
spiced meat holes,

patois Sunday
chances lost,
for hair-weave girls
and mouths of gold.

Burkas mix
with tracksuit gobs
and kids on scooters
learn to fly

past tram stops
and each paper shop,
curbs of
random paradise.

Tandoor sunset
frames the day,
dark window movie
presentations,

trailers for a
fruit stall magic,
circus colouring
ripe sensations.

A parade of citrus,
white teeth smiles,
in themes of
burst kaleidoscope,

to moments kept
in slot machines
tied with bits of
skipping rope.

In a market where
stretched canvas wraps
the bartering soliloquy,

a disused pub for
money changers,
knock-off jeans
and hosiery.

Crossings
are for decoration,
piano keys
for cars to play,

traffic lights are
incidental,
lanterns for the
come what may.

Shadows slip into
the cracks
dusk falls onto
road's warm skin,

a cinnamon
dusted candy neon,

place to keep your spirit in.

AMANI SAEED
I WAS TOLD TO WRITE MY OWN TRUTHS...

I was told to write my own truths:
somehow, being brown is always one of them.
But I don't want to tell you about being a "brown girl."
I don't speak for "brown girls," because
like we assume white individuality, how we separate
their shades of pearl, alabaster, cream
there are different shades of chai, coffee, and teak.

When I speak, I speak for me.
And let me tell you, I get culture shock
every time I look in the mirror.

I'm not an ABCD or a BBCD, I'm more of a
British-born, American-raised, confused as hell desi except
I've got some other ancestry mixed
in me but I can never be sure of what it is
because my grandma lost our copy of the family tree—
fuck me.

When god made me, he took the teabag out too early.
Omnipotent deity didn't listen to auntieji
and strained the tea leaves too quickly
when he made his morning cup of chai,
tried to find a way to avoid wastage
and instead painted my skin with it.

Now I'm basted this semi-toasted tint that I can't name,
holding up a pantone color chart and praying
my shade's on there somewhere.

So birthed into this world with my stained skin
I'm asked the inevitable question: "Where do you really come from?"
As if I know.

While my brown friends call India the motherland,
I think I must be adopted—
how could it be my motherland if it didn't birth me,
if I've never seen it firsthand?

Shoutout to Salman Rushdie for teaching me
that my homeland is imaginary.
Cause it really ain't my homeland, ain't even
my mother's homeland, ain't even
my mother's mother's homeland, not really.

Nanijan was taken from India at fifteen and arranged
into a marriage with a full grown man.
Kenya the next homeland for my mother,
then Hounslow, brownsville of London,
in an attached house with pink walls where I was born
and then brought to America, homeland number three.

Now I've got this accent, these friendships,
this family that spans oceans, ancestry that circles the whole globe
I am proof that the whole world is home.
That this world is borderless.
There's nobody who can tell me what I am
because there's nobody who can tell me what I'm not:

I span hot desert winds and Hyderabadi biriyani,
calligraphic inscriptions and swimming competitions,
scones with clotted cream and jam and advanced placement exams,
shalwar kameez that love my curved hips and Abercrombie
jeans that just won't sit over them, masala dosas,
samosas and mimosas, Arabic lessons,
Saturday detentions, text messages, varsity jackets,
empty Cadbury packets,
I am one international, multicultural package
wrapped up in brown paper and tied up with white string
my song is strewn all over this earth.

So you better believe that next time
anyone asks me where I really come from,
I'll just tell them

I come from home.

JAMES BUNTING
BONES

This life is a bonfire of yesterdays —
it's a tried and tested method
of losing our ways
among the streets of this city we love.
But it's the same sky above;
same as it's always been
the only thing that will listen to your eyes scream
when the slow walkers and fast talkers get a hold of you
but there is more to this city that we wander through,
more to the houses and the homes.
And it's you, city, you're the one who shaped me —
drew lay-lines on my bones and sang lullabies to me —
when the rain fell, we laughed in it;
and when the sun shone, we danced in it;
and when we stood on top of that tower to watch the sun set
we saw the light splash down making the leaves wet.

It's a different thing to look down on what you love;
it's a different thing to be above it all
tracing maps from where you first fell in love
to where you went to school,
but it's a world we all should know:
where the heart beats fast and your eyes blink slow.
It's the paradise we dream of finding;
it's the burning world beyond the horizon
where everything is as it's meant to be
and nothing can hurt you,
nothing can hurt me.
Though we're just strangers,
that doesn't mean I don't love you
because the same fire that burns in me burns in you too.
I can see it, when you look directly at me.
Catch the falling light soaking the trees we stand above.
You remember what I said about love?

It's in the city I grew up in.
It's in the people I've watched growing
into human beings I could cling to,
when the rain sets in I'll give shelter to,
but if you should just find my skeleton picked clean as stones,
you'll find a map of Bristol etched upon my bones.

Lead me to the edge. Let's dare each other to fall
because a life not lived properly
that's not a proper life at all,
and we owe it to the stars, you know,
we owe it to the moon,
because they're the ones who're watching us
dancing through the room.
This life is fleeting,
this life is brief,

but it's fear of these two facts
that people get so scared about
they wind up calling belief.
Me? I'm just a traveller,
with dust upon my shoes,
because you can walk forever
when you've nothing left to lose,
and age is just what happens when you live a life so full
that when you stop to look at time
you realise you've no time at all.

But this city will always cradle me,
from my first love to my last,
from the day I realised the world could change
to standing up here on this stage
watching prophecies come to pass.
It's not a devil that I'm dancing with
it's the sound of my mother's voice,
teaching me the rights and wrongs,
all the words to all the songs,
and that you always have a choice.
And to some that might sound scary
because it's the way you change your life;
to realise there's just two things you can't prevent:
the tide and the night.

And the night is already here now,
you can see it shot full of stars,
so I'll walk down to the beach alone
leave behind the sound of cars.
And the stars reflect in the water,
my father always told me they're the moon's sons
and the sun's daughters
and I don't burn as bright as them,
that's just not the way that I was born,
so, I'll flip a coin in the sand,
fix up how I'm torn between staying here or going
back to the city I love
where I can walk the familiar streets
with demons below and angels above.
And the fates can stand on every corner,
fixing me with a stare,
I'll just drop my eyes and walk on by,
cover my ears to the distant screams and the muffled prayers.

I don't have much for you,
but I can promise you one thing:
if you look for me on the beach, I'll show you the tide
bright and sparkling;
if we look up we'll see the clouds begin to turn;
and if we wait for long enough we'll see the horizon burn;
but when you get there,
if you should just find my skeleton,
picked clean as stones,
you'll find a map of Bristol etched upon my bones.

LUCY ENGLISH
THE TELEPHONE BOX UP ASHLEY HILL

There's a telephone box up Ashley Hill
where I go and stand sometimes when I'm feeling down.
From up there I can see the allotments sloping
towards the terraced grid of houses in St. Werburghs
and the streets of Easton, Eastville and beyond,
the frst felds just outside Bath. The ridge of hills

reminding me that the city isn't endless.
However stuck and messed up I feel,
when I stand there I know there are places
I haven't been to yet,
and people I don't know at all
are waiting for me as surely
as the clump of trees up Kelston Hill.

There's a telephone box up Ashley Hill
where I go and stand sometimes when I'm feeling down.
Because I've been in the rain up there.
When the rain dripped off my nose
and the hills disappeared in the clouds.
And I've been in the sun up there,
watching the heat rise off the dusty city.
and I've seen the view so winter white.
The curving hills like frosted crystal.

And I've been drunk up there.
Watching the stars slide across the sky.
And I've tripped up there.
Going to the moon with a ten pence piece.
And I've been up there with lovers
Kissing passionately banging against the phone box.
Or just held hands in silence
watching the sky grow red with sunsets.
And once and only once
I landed up in the nettles
in a dope fuelled tangle of lust.
Don't try it. I had a rash for days

And a long time ago
I took a little boy up there
and we hung onto the railings
our coats flapping in the wind.
The spring wind pressing our eyeballs tight.
And I shouted, "Look, look at the view!"
And he looked, a solemn old man four year old
and said, "The sky is very big."

There's telephone box up Ashley Hill
where I go and stand sometimes when I'm feeling down.
To look at the view
and the big sky.

EMMA JOLIFFE
SW2: GENTRIFICATION POEM

The chicken shop
was garish,
its strip lights flickered
and the cartoon chicken
inexplicably
wore a gangster hat
but every Friday
families sat
with sticky hot wings,
chips drowned in sauce;
through the windows
I saw them.

And then it was gone,
another boarded-up building,
another licence pinned up
fluttering in the wind.
Then the new restaurant
was being fitted, measured,
built in,

and the street art
was of Tupac, Biggie, Nas,
their faces loomed large
on the shutters
which rolled up to reveal
a brand new concept
'Hip-Hop Chip Shop',
champagne
and squid.

It's funny
'cause now I only see white faces inside,
it's financial apartheid,
another space
where those Somali families
can't sit
and the irony
of using black faces
to trendify it.

LAURIE BOLGER
THE TARTED-UP BOOZER IN SHOREDICH

We ditched the familiar smell
of stale beer and sodden bar towels
for a molten-orange glowing counter top
with BAR written in neon lights
on top of a fish-tank, home to five
of the most miserable marine creatures
I had ever seen, poor boozy bar fish
taking it all in.

We ditched the rabble and the riot
of our West End local
for a bunch of moody indie kids
with shit haircuts and boardgames
rolling cigarettes and posing
as the singer/actor/part-time model –
girls in green Barbour coats
with bird-nest hair
sipping brown ale,
they'd like a Bacardi Breezer secretly
and they burn incense sticks
so you can barely tell your pint
from sandalwood.

We ditched our plump busty landlady
who sweats under bright lights
and breathes heavy as she pulls me a pint.
We ditched her for an indie cindie barman
dressed in Grandad-style knitwear,
a dickie-bow tie
and Topshop's finest pair of thick black glasses
too big for his face.

You look a bit like Jarvis Cocker, mate,
and those are not prescription lenses
in those frames.

He's mechanic and uncharming,
looks alarmed when I ask him,
'What's your cheapest pint, mate?'
He tells me, 'We only do
bottles of beer and they're all, like,

four pounds.'
It's all very dark,
we take in
the candlelit ambience,
with a mannequin,
a moose head wearing a top hat,
and lampshades like my nan had.

The DJ is dropping beats
behind the smallest DJ booth
I've ever seen.
Next to the gents'
he's working the decks,
like he's working
the crowd at Creamfields.
Everyone is sat down.

I begin to miss the local pub's jukebox mix
of punk, funk, folk, the occasional Irish,
the locals' sing-song, soles beating
the battered carpet.

This place has the slipperiest floor
I have ever walked across
and I'm wearing high shoes
'cause it's a little bit posh here.

I slide into the loos
where girls paint pretentious stares
and flick their hair and look really,
genuinely, actually posh.

We go and do some shots
with indie boy Jarvis, who's still
one hundred percent deadpan.

He doesn't tell us his life story
like the old bloke in our local,
and I could spend a year here
trying to meet an old friend,
or create something humble,
but we leave because it's shit.

We ramble home through city drizzle,
street lights make puddles jaundice-yellow
and I can breathe again.

Paraffin-blue lights
cut through dark
and make me jump,
so I climb onto the night bus,
take my shoes off,
and travel across this tourist town,

to our grubby little local,
just around the corner,

where we know
we are guaranteed
to get a lock-in.

PENNY PEPPER
BUS

On the bus
Boris bus
dirty bumpy
horrid bus.

There's a trolley in the crip space –
see the child, snotty faced –
bullish buggy hellish mummy
disposition far from sunny.

On the bus
double decker
smelly shaky
bony wrecker.

There's a suitcase in the crip space
nervous girl who grips in haste
snarling hoodie chomping burger
Doesn't he know that meat is murder?

On the bus
Boris bus
dirty bumpy
horrid bus.

Another journey, ramp is broken
access just an empty token?
Public selfish, my dismay,
while driver grunts and looks away.

On the bus
double decker
smelly bumpy
bony wrecker.

In my slot a man with doggy –
by my shoulder youth who's groggy
armpits foul, hair is stinking
smells of vomit, and binge drinking.

On the bus
Boris bus
dirty bumpy
horrid bus.

There we were such humble cripples,
fought the system sent out ripples –
now to take a London bus
with the throng to push to fuss –

On the bus
Boris bus
dirty bumpy
Tory bus
any bus
big or small
dirty rough
crowded empty
loud and surly…

Scarcely,
Just a London
Bus
Not
Much
fucking
Use to us.

KATE FOX
OUR ENDS IN THE NORTH

On the first day the world ended,
I said "Least said soonest mended.
"Sometimes these things are sent to try us."
Though in this case, they were sent to fry us.
But in the North we don't like to make a fuss us,
though sometimes, I admit, we make a bit of a fuss
about how we don't make a fuss.
In fact that "No Fuss Festival"
with the new play by Alan Bennett
"Not Fussed"
and the 38 act opera "Unfussy"
starring Lesley "I Never Make A Fuss Me" Garrett
might, upon reflection
have constituted making a fuss.
But just because it's Doomsday, there's no need to make
a big song and dance about it.
On the second day I was on the bus
when there was a bang and all the lights went out–
and there was a chorus,
of "Call this an Apocalypse? I felt nowt".
and "Grimsby hasn't looked this good since
the Germans redecorated."
You've got to make the best of things,
Northerners are tough like that
nobody else compares.
On the third day, the Tyne Bridge fell into a crack
in the space-time continuum
I said "I'll go to the foot of our stairs",
but when I got home, there weren't any.
On the fourth day,
Cleckheaton exploded.
I said "Worse things happen at sea."
and popped on a Bear Grylls DVD.
On the fifth day the government said it was tough for everyone,
with it being the Apocalypse
but that actually in London the restaurants were full
and maybe we just weren't trying hard enough
in Liverpool, Newcastle and Hull.

We should get on our bikes
and there not being any roads left, or bikes, was just an excuse.
On the sixth day, the streets were full of people wandering about,
moaning.
The Zombies hadn't come–
it was just folk complaining about the price of petrol
and how the Co Op had run out of white sliced.
On the seventh day Greggs' Ham and Armageddon pasties
were going down a storm,
and they didn't have to charge tax
as the surface radiation kept them warm.
On the eighth day there were no planes in the sky,
we had street parties,
shared the last of our tins,
best china was brought out, bunting unfurled.
Armageddon?
What's the problem? we said,
"It's not the end of the world."

JEMIMA FOXTROT
(FROM ALL DAMN DAY)

I wish, I wish but it's all in vain,
I wish I was a maid again
but a maid again I never can be
'til apples grow on the orange tree.

I'm lying down with my family.   And we are here in the height
of July on a Scottish, not so hot, pebbled beach.
                        But the sun is out.

The littlest of my nieces, six and seven, are running around
in nothing but knickers, their dry cozzies rejected,
squashed at the bottom of our bags,

they're scurrying after crabs, chasing the incoming tide away,
            squealing in ripples like piglets,
getting high off the natural light,
            off the summer, off the seaside.

I wish, I wish.

They're lured back to our picnic blanket
by strawberries and apple juice and sandwiches
that have somehow got sand in them
and warm dry adult hugs
and ice cream from the van that plays
if you go down to the woods today...

Further down the beach   two older girls, about ten or
eleven, stretch out,   apprentice lionesses on beach towels,
pull giant sunglasses down on their eyes
            (so they look like flies) as they try to wisely sigh.

They behave in a way that says,
'Check me, I am doing what grown-ups do on a beach.
Check me, I might not be one but I am a teenager
and I'm doing what teenagers do,
you may think I'm just a child but you haven't got a clue.'

One of my little ones stops running, pot-bellied in damp pants,
and looks.

Next day, well rested and hot-chocolated and ready
for play on the beach again, it's different.
They scramble to the bottom of the bags,
chuck out the buckets and spades

and put their swimming costumes on.

Within the minute, they're laughing and splashing,
        still piglets.

I have witnessed this, in one swift moment like a photograph,
this sudden crumbling of their sweet and childish
        lack of self-consciousness like a conquered city's wall.

I have witnessed this, this milestone,
this shift in their visions that will never shift back.

I have just witnessed their rough innocence collapsing

and an origamied womanhood will grow
from their souls in its place.

I wish, I wish but it's all in vain,
I wish I was a maid again
but a maid again I never can be
'til apples grow on the orange tree.

SOPHIA BLACKWELL
THE FIRE EATER'S LOVER

BOYS

SALLY JENKINSON

Laurie Bolger
Box Rooms

HANNAH M. TEASDALE
LAID BARE

James Bunting
onkers

ALL DAMN DAY

JEMIMA FOXTROT

still falling
sara hirsch

includes the viral hit 'Watchland' viewed 300,000 times on YouTube
HAPPINESS IS AN ART FORM
Award-winning Poetry about the science of happiness

AGNES TOROK

BADMINTON

MOLLY NAYLOR

LETTERS I NEVER SENT TO YOU
Poetry & Prose 2007 - 2016
by Paula Varjack

Little Boy Blue
Jamal Mehmood

ELVIS McGONAGALL
VIVA LOCH LOMOND

CRUMBS FROM A SPINNING WORLD

CRYSSE MORRISON

Selah
Keith Jarrett

¿Who Knows?

Jeremy Toombs

MOLLY CASE
NURSING THE NATION

A woman comes in,
too young to bear this;
she's got a disease that will make her miss –
her daughter's wedding day,
her first grandchild being born.
How would that feel, to have that all torn
away from you?

I can't answer that question,
it's not my place to say,
but I can tell you what we did for her,
how we helped her get through the day.
A cup of tea there and one for all her family,
as they came, throughout the night,
what a sight; there were loads of them.
To help her fight the awful pain of it,
paying last visits, we wouldn't let them miss it –
farewell from a brother,
last kisses with their mother –
holiest love, love like no other.

Maybe there's bad ones,
no doubt that there are,
but for this list I'm writing
we don't want the same tar-brush,
crushing our careers before they've even started;
how could you say this
about people so big-hearted?
Who would have thought we'd be having to defend?
We don't do this for our families,
we don't do this for our friends,
but for strangers.
Because this is our vocation
and we're sick and tired
of being told we don't do enough for this nation.
So listen to us, hear us goddamn roar;
you say we're not doing enough?
Then we promise we'll do more.
This time, next time,

there's nothing we can't handle,
even if you bring us down,
show us scandal, scandal, scandal.

You remember that man covered in burns head to toe?
I don't think you do
'cause you were on that TV show:
lipgloss-kissed women on daytime TV,
come into our world, see things that we see.

One lady, passing, had no relatives to stay.
We sang her to sleep, let angels take her away.
Were you there that day when we held her hand?
Told her nothing would harm her,
that there was a higher plan.
Saw her face as she remembered a faith she'd once held,
watched her breath in the room as she finally exhaled.

Why don't you meet us? Come, shake our hands.
Try to fit it in between having tea with your fans.
Your hands are so soft and mine are cracked.
Why don't you let us on air?
Let us air the facts.

We've washed and shrouded people
that we've never known,
pinned flowers to the sheet
and told them they're still not alone.
Shown families to the faith room
and watched them mourn their dead,
then got back to work, bathed patients, made beds.

Hindus, Muslims, Jews and Sikhs,
Buddhists and Christians and just people off the street,
we've cared for them all and we love what we do,
we don't want a medal, we just want to show you.
So listen to us, hear us goddamn roar;
you say we're not doing enough?
Then we promise we'll do more.

ELVIS MCGONAGALL
THAT GOVERNMENT HEALTHCARE POLICY IN FULL

Denigrate, degrade, defenestrate
Compassion's past its sell-by-date
Wave farewell to the Welfare State
Let the poor die

Demonise, deride, demoralise
Carve it all up, cut it down to size
Follow the profit, privatise
Let the poor die

Carry on doctor 24/7
All good nurses go to heaven
Don't need a new Aneurin Bevan
Just let the poor die

Alcopop-pizza-doughnut guts
Varicose veins, cigarette butts
Lousy lifestyle choices – tut, tut tut
Let the poor die

It's Charlie Darwin's natural selection
Healthy, wealthy Ubermenschen
Survival of the fittest pension
Let the poor die

Caring's simply too intensive
Pharmaceuticals – so expensive
Sign up for cover that's comprehensive
Let the poor die

No more needy "patients" in despair
You're valued customers of Virgin Care
Got no insurance? Say a little prayer
Let the poor die

Virgin Upper Class illness won't cost the earth
Choose Virgin syphilis, get your money's worth
Call the Virgin Midwife for a Virgin birth
Let the poor die

Three heart transplants for the price of two
Fast food surgery – drive on through
In an ambulance run by Deliveroo
Let the poor die

Pay for an Extra Special prognosis
The Finest drugs and diagnosis
Truly Irresistible tuberculosis
Let the poor die

Basic Saver service for the tightwad sod
Competitively priced, not too slipshod
Meet your consultant Mr Sweeney Todd
Let the poor die

Take an aspirin for your cancer
Call your local necromancer
Waiting room full? Here's the answer
Let the poor die

Depression is mere melancholy
Pull out that drip, get off that trolley
Beds are for clients with loadsa lolly
Let the poor die

Do something for nothing? Keep the receipt
Altruism is obsolete
NHS? New Harley Street
Let the poor die

Drown yourself in blood, sweat, tears and toil
Silently shuffle off this mortal coil
Shovelled six feet under Virgin soil
Let the poor die

Hey presto! No money! Disappearing trick
Dismantling our hospitals brick by brick
It's this government that's fucking sick
They'll just let the poor die

JESS GREEN
BURNING BOOKS

I work in a school library
with a woman who reads different papers to me,
papers that shout through open doors
then scarper down the Science block
when Mr Peters comes.
Papers that hold back the fear
with a strut and a sway
and a spit at the little kids
and call the Polish boys poofs,
rip the middle pages out of their books.
Papers that admit in empty classrooms
at half past three
that they don't know when Dad's getting out
and that makes their lips and fists shake
when they look at me.

She recounts these scared stories
with feigned intrigue
like on her first day
when she seemed friendly
and I was pleased
having typed away
in an empty room since January.

She sat down and said,
'Have you heard the news?'
I waited,
breath bated,
for her views
on Italian elections,
press reform,
HIV cures,
who to vote for Pope
and how many people died in Iran on Monday.

But all of that
paled in comparison
to Pippa Middleton's yellow coat,
boys marrying grandmothers in somewhere not English,
capital letters of arson and attack
and none of it deserved,
the Queen's diarrhoea,
Prince Charles smiling,

another one drinking,
Kate Middleton's hat,
and 'She's pregnant, did you hear that she's pregnant?'

In between these fleeting tastes
of the world outside
the books and the walls
she plays the lottery,
says it's her only toe dip
into accountancy
but her luck's coming up,
she can feel it,
that change on the breeze;
she'd never give it to charity, though,
I mean,
who can you trust?
You don't know what they'd do with it.
She took over the books
like conquering land
with the plastic cubes in Risk.
She said there were too many,
took them to the tip
in boxes that got caught
in the boot of her car,
they were piled so high.

The ones that were left?
Well, the kids don't treat them
the way she wants them to treat them.
Like the girl who never wears her tie or blazer,
pug-faced from indignation,
told 'There's no time for you,
go back to class,'
but she can't go back empty-handed
so she slaps a grab
at Horrid Henry volume three
but the librarian quick to save her loot
smacks her palm down
to protect it.

Skin on skin.
All those *Daily Mail* headlines
paste the walls
and I see her imprinted in every one
as the girl explodes into tears
and looks at me.

'Miss?'
Question mark.
'Go back to class.'

There are statements half-heartedly taken
and I don't lie,
I just keep quiet,
but nothing comes of it
because everyone's too terrified
of anything coming of it.

World Book Day comes
with a briefcase and a suit,
he hands me his coat,
tells me his coffee's too strong
and instructs the kids to silence
with the story of his tie
because his tie's got a TARDIS on
but none of the kids
know what a TARDIS is
because Matt Smith is out
and the plot got too tough
and, 'Sir, when can we go?
I hate books.'

He's stunned.
Clenching his knuckles
like clutching a Michael Gove report,
he spits
this kid better get used to it,
give education a year
and it'll be 'Charge of the Light Brigade'
by heart
and then he'll know how life can be hard.

All the bright lights of World Book Day fade
and a fight in the corridor
pulls down a poster of Tony Robinson's face.

Her expressions change so quickly.
She's slagging off Sita in the office
for chewing too loudly
chewing too often
chewing the wrong thing
then Sita walks in
and she grins,
starts bitching about the kids,

because they're always there,
they laugh too much,
fart too much,
look at her too much
like they want something.
Why do they always want something?
What do they want?

I only work part-time
so I only hear half of this.
It's the kids who get the full show.

At lunch, she tells me how her diet is better than mine,
I say, 'I'm not on one,'
she doesn't care,
hers is about
only eating lettuce only eating things that are yellow
only eating on days that begin with an s or a t
and never eating
when she's always eating
and, 'Jess, have you noticed how Sita in the office
is always eating?'

She'll try anything to keep the kids out,
herd them back down the English block,
she stands at the door
dictating faces that can pass
on a promise that they'll
'Sit in silence,
speak when spoken to,
not make themselves noticeable
and not touch the books.'

'If you want one,
you take it.
Don't peruse;
don't fiddle;
don't read the blurb,
decide it's not for you,
then replace it back on the wrong shelf.
Don't bring it back
torn
folded
wet
enjoyed
crinkled

thumbed
carried in a rucksack for a week
to find any opportunity
just to love it in a stairwell or under a desk.'

If they do, they get a letter home,
a ransom note.
It's her favourite part of the day,
rattling off addresses
announcing how unsurprised she is
that Megan brought back Tracy Beaker
two days late,
being from that corner of the estate.
Then Megan's banned for two weeks,
when she protests it becomes a month
and a stamp of her foot
and the word 'bitch'
under her breath
gets her a life sentence.

This is Megan who loves books,
she's got an imagination you can drown in
and now she just hangs around outside
sticking her chewing gum in the windows
of the canteen
and she glares at me.
One day, the Deputy Head pulls me in,
tells me it's my job to get them

in between the pages,
picking up books.

She gives me a job title with the word 'Champion' in it
and targets to meet by Christmas.
I'm walking back along the fourth-period corridor,
through the double doors,
she is in between two piles,
the shelves are bare.
One tower's near toppling,
reaching the panelled ceiling,
the other one's barely up to her knees.

'What are you doing?' I say.
She's up like I'm going to tell on her.
'Do you know how much filth is in this room?'

she says.
She's picking up titles from the highest pile,
throwing them in the bin
with the juice packets
and the apple cores,
listing their faults
like it's my fault.

'*The Kite Runner,*
rape and buggery.
Adrian Mole,
masturbation.
Jane Eyre,
woman kept hostage against her will.
White Teeth,
cult religion.
Black Beauty,
bestiality.
Time Traveler's Wife,
sex with a minor.
Macbeth,
too violent.

Regeneration,
too gay.
Great Gatsby,
too much drinking.
DH Lawrence,
don't get me started.

'It's all over the headlines,'
she says.
'Kids aren't safe on streets
and in schools
and these books are like bombs
turning teenagers into weapons
filling their heads
with dirt and desire
and I will not sit back
and watch this country go to rot.'

MARK GRIST
A TEACHER, EH?

The starter's removed.
The main course emerges.
And when I'm asked what I do for a living
our host's reaction verges
on the incredulous.
Half-digested food that's been fed to us
spittoons from his lips.
He leans in, snarls and quips,
'A teacher, eh?

Wouldn't catch me wasting my time
with today's youth.
Just a bunch of grubby little shits!'
The wolves laugh around him,
applaud the wit that he just fired.
His wife smoothes my arm like it's tablecloth,
she says, 'No wonder he looks so tired!'
The room erupts again and I laugh too
because she's right.
I am tired.

I'm tired from days spent
saying, 'Tuck in that shirt.'
From getting kids into lines,
and making girls unroll their skirts.
I'm tired from setting tests
to the grumbling and complaining.
Exams get me stressed.
Giving detentions can be draining.
And who'd have guessed it'd be so tiring
making lessons entertaining?
The kids don't care, 'cause someone's farted
or had a nosebleed
or it's just raining.

And I'm tired from working with artists,
with athletes, with dancers.

I'm tired from asking questions
'til I realise I don't know all the answers,
and then I'm tired from watching the sparks that
fly behind young eyes.
The heroes born in the classroom.
The self-worth they realise.
And then those other kids

where you have to tie on a line,
dive deep inside,
rescue the shreds of confidence
another adult rusted up inside.
I'm tired from scrabbling at those locks,
dredging back those pearls,
then saying, 'Well done, I'll see you next week.'
Letting them back out into the world.
I'm tired of teaching Year 8 boys
that flirting isn't just kicking girls.

And I'm tired of working with young people
who invest in their community
who aren't happy accepting
our grown-up mediocrity.
And while the efforts of the majority sink
to the back of the local paper,
the one kid with a blade who hates the world
because nobody taught him better
gets plastered on page one,
so when I am tired, when our work is all done
I get to stand on duty, watching adults' fearful looks
directed at my young minds, laughing
as they travel home with their books.
But look. Mostly right now I'm tired
because yesterday in class
we were discussing poverty in Uganda.
Throughout it my students were irate,
raw with anger.

They just couldn't understand the fact that young people
are starving in our world by the score.
And when one girl asked me, 'Sir. How can this happen?
How can you adults let the poor stay poor?'
It got me thinking all night about what I once stood for.

So, yeah, you may all be successful.
This meal may well be Michelin.
But I'd swap the swine around me now
for a dozen kids on Ritalin,
'cause those 'grubby little shits'
won't learn your layers of indifference.
And I am tired. I'm exhausted.
But teaching's what I do.
I feed others before I feed myself
so that (fingers crossed)
I never become
as overfed as you.

NASSER HUSSAIN
BUSINESS SPEAK

I'm so close to the means of my production I can smell it. coffee tastes a bit like sweat. the lucid limit of my language. the plastic limit of my overdraft. da doo doo doo, da da da da, that's all I want to scat at you. they call it scat for a reason, but there is no reckoning three hours into a meeting, between floors, or buckled in for the takeoff. my ass is the means of my morning production. the relief of everything I eat. all labour runs to scat. all bacon strips in the end. chit-chat about cat shit. a ruined duvet and the effort to care. pain is a vertical index of humour. the more it hurts, the more we laugh, slapsticks in unison. groins tighten in dark theatres. a piece of work can't get much closer than that. if it looks like a hershey kiss, walks like a hershey kiss, talks like a hershey kiss, don't trust it my friend. I said don't trust it because you are my friend even though I don't like you. the best way to make friends is to make friendly. the leeward calmer seemingly. but the wind is the collected farts of a ruminate planet, and it's easy to confuse a new idea with breaking wind. in elevators especially. it wasn't me, I'm thinking, and you know it's true since I am the friendly sort. I quit producing before I came to work this morning, so it couldn't be.

MOLLY NAYLOR
THINGS SAID TO ME IN MEETINGS WITH TELEVISION EXECUTIVES

Can you just change the gays a bit?
Hugo has never met gays like these.
Trouble is, there just aren't any black directors.
I like your shoes, are they from the nineties?
Norwich... is that in Cornwall?

We're not really doing subtle this year,
we did too much subtle last year.
Do people actually work in fruit and veg shops, though?
I need you to make this 35% funnier.
Can you use your Oyster card in Norwich?

As a working class guy from Walton-on-the-Naze,
I really relate to this character's struggle.
Not that my parents were unemployed
and I mean our house was pretty big
but that was only because my gran died.

Gay is so hot this year
bi is so hot this year
trans is so hot this year
refugees are so right now
whereabouts in London is Norwich?

Thing is, men don't watch female shows.
Women watch male shows
because there aren't many female shows.
What's more millennial, a high-five or a fist-bump?
Listen, I just don't feel that she's a lesbian.

It's Girls, but with boys,
it's Jurassic Park meets Brookside,
it's The Apprentice meets Five Children and It,
it's Jaws, but if Jaws was a man and the sea was all women.
Norwich? Is that where that guy is from?

Hugo's still not convinced by the gays...
what if one of them was a tap-dancer?
Can we make her mixed-race as a compromise?
People won't watch it if she's in a wheelchair.

You said you didn't want a coffee, didn't you?
Keep sending us stuff, won't you?
Back to Norwich, then, is it?
Where did you say that was?

DAN SIMPSON
CLICKBAIT

After The First Line Of This Poem
You'll Never Believe What Happens Next
Three Lines In I Was Completely Hooked
And That Thing You Assumed To Be True?
Well, If You Only Do One Thing Today
Make Sure It's Read To The End Of This Poem
Only The Most Awesome People Do This
This Is One Poem You Should Not Miss
After All, Does This Leading Question
Lead To Anything Significant?
Find Out After The Line Break.

You Need To See What This Poem Does Next
This Poem, Made By A Five-Year Old Kid
Who Is Way Wiser Than Most Adults
Because There's 26 Things
Only People Who See This Poem Will Understand
If You Thought It Was Clickbait? Think Again
I Mean, What Kind Of Poetry Person Are You?
Watch This Poem Move Across The Page To Find Out
Or Listen To This Celebrity Reading This Poem
As The Shocking Truth Hits Home
For One Reason And One Reason Only:
Click Me. Share Me. Love Me.

Learn How To Write Something Like This In Just 12 Seconds
Meet The Words Behind Some Of The Most Successful Poems
Of All Time
The Results Are Completely Unexpected
As 9 Weird Things About Poetry You Didn't Know Till Now
Are Explained By This One Guy
Who Makes A Powerful Point So Eloquently
It Will Somehow Change The World
And You Will Cry Or Laugh Or Shrug
Before Clicking On The Next Poem
Which Is All About Miley Cyrus.

Let's Talk About How This Poem Speaks To You
And The Way That Little Words Can Have Huge Impact
This Is Why Most People Don't Get Poetry
And The Next Time Someone Says To You

Pretty Much Anything About Poetry
Just Link Them To This Poem
Like It Applies To Every Conversation
Answers Every Question You Ever Had About Anything.

What Kind Of 90s Feminist Sandwich Filling Disney Character
Are You?
Take This Poem To Find Out.

Wait Till You See What This Poem Has To Say
I Dare You To Look At This Poem And Not Think: "What?"
And Usually You'd Be Right
But Prepare To Have Your Mind Blown
This Poem Has An Important Message
That Everyone Should See
And It Will Inspire You
It Will Inspire You
It Will Inspire You
It Will Inspire You
Or Not.
Just Click It. Share It. Love It.

SOPHIA BLACKWELL
MIXTAPES

I miss them – don't you? Those long Sunday nights
hanging over the arm of your parents' sofa,
itchy fingers poised for the end of the track.
You were an explorer, mapping from front to back,
marching into that vacuum, that white-noise hiss.
You were a general, marshalling ranks of rock stars
all in your quest to get that single kiss.

The language of tapes was pure interpretation.
Songs were the flags you hid your face behind.
Your telegraphed semaphore blurring the lines,
fast-forwarding in a falsetto whine,
Pause. Skip. Rewind. Tongue-tied, through the wires,
desperate as only teenagers can be.
Hear me. Pick me. Play. Click. Go. Only connect.

I miss them. Don't you? Sure, now it's quick and clean,
no end of space, no ninety-minute calculations,
and yes, there's beauty even in downloaded data,
your memory banks decanted in an hourglass.
There's still the thought, the careful lettering,
but no matter what, it's not really a party thing,
not a careful labour of love looped on a shoestring.

And I miss that kind of love, the fan-dance of belonging.
Hard to see it go, to see the tapes you own,
those stacks of lovers' gifts and nothing that'll play them.
The buzz, the fillers, those ridiculous dates –
Mix 96. 99. 01. Go on. Say them. Don't grieve
for what you both believed. Play. Go. Fast-forward.
Pause. See that single crooked heart on the sleeve.

AMY MCALLISTER
THE THINGS I OWN THAT DON'T BELONG TO ME

Winking soldier in the poppy photo frame,
I hold you here
To keep my hands from looking lonely.
To fill my room with history.
My complicated reason to own an extra pillow.
I do a bit of acting when the postman comes,
Am sure to leave my lips an open bracket,
My eyes a dot-dot-dot...
But you always did prefer that boy to me.
You're probably shacked up
In the Dominican Republic.
For as long as I keep up the show of waiting,
I can drink the quenching flow of sympathy.
It washes down the frozen meals the neighbours leave
Which taste of salt, and self-congratulation.
Lasagne dishes, bowls, and clip-lock Tupperware
Pile up like bodies in a lazy grave,
The batons in a one-man relay race
From fridge to hob to chair to sink to fridge again.
I pick my slippered feet above
A knee-high maze of articles and cuttings:
Bloody, fact-filled, hand-delivered love letters
From helpful friends.
And then there are the women from the factory
Who bring me scarves and slips,
Some pretty gown the foreman's overlooked,
Hoping we can all get all dolled up and hit the town.
Our house so empty and so full of you,
Of all the things I own that don't belong to me.

STEF MO
SMALL TALK

I wish things weren't so awkward.
We've faced apocalypses together, stood
shoulder to bleeding shoulder
backs to bloodied wall
facing down howling hordes, armed
with nothing
but bruised fsts
shit-eating grins
and camaraderie
yet sit us together in the same living room
with an afternoon to kill
and it's like a frst date between two people
who are only doing it
because they share some really pushy mutual friends.
I spend too much time fddling
with tea and coffee-making paraphernalia
and you keep sort-of-but-not-really reading
an old Guardian Culture section
and small talk chokes and chugs
like an old machine
and I watch dying cells dive off my arm
like the last hurrah of some suicide cult
and I still can't remember if you take sugar.
So we end up just... sitting.
And if anyone asked, I know we'd both swear the silence
is companionable
although we both know it really, really isn't
and I don't think I've ever been more relieved
to see a grenade hurtling through an open window.
God
I think I was actually just about to ask you
something about football.

SARA HIRSCH
EPILOGUE

My feet are falling away from me.
Four months and six plane rides later
and I haven't moved from your side.
I stood between your brother and mine
in deliberate, unplanned retaliation
at the rules of the room.

Women stand on the left
and the men read from the right:
backwards, if you ask me. She
stroked the whitened shroud
like the times I never saw her
hold your hand. Like in eighty years

she had never touched sadness
as soft as that. Her knuckles cracked,
her voice followed suit: Well, goodbye, then.
And my feet fell. My soles met yours
and they danced together, briefly,
like the times you never

let me stand on your shoes
and you never spun me round
while Nana never clapped
and smiled sunshine from the corner.
I am still walking away from that silence.
I will always be falling away from the time

I couldn't say goodbye. I could still taste
the last time I tried. It was as solid as a
hospital meal on a dehydrated tongue
and the promise you made that you would
see me again is still dripping into my bloodstream
like nutrients I didn't know I didn't need.

FERGUS MCGONIGAL
ELEGY ON THE THINGS WE NEVER KNEW
For my fellow adoptees

Don't try and keep the past alive: it's long
since dead. Place a sign around its neck:
Do not resuscitate. Burn photographs
you never had, whose faces you will never see.
Inter home movies which you never watched
in some dark, silent tomb marked Not For Me.
The Christmas cards, the birthday presents, none
of which were bought or sent, the family jokes
you never heard, the memories you never shared,
the holidays you never took, the homes
in which you never slept, the promises
you never made, or tried to keep, or never kept,
the loving words which went unsaid, the absent hands
which never touched a single hair upon
your precious head; and all the things that never were
and all the things that might have been: take them all!
and drown them in the ocean of your grief.

Do not look forward yet: the future is
as unknown as the past you never knew.
Instead, be here. Breathe. Live. Love. Laugh. Don't stop..

KESHIA STARRETT
ULTRASOUND

As I crowned I saw   a slice   at the
end of her; an exit wound that can't or   won't   heal,
which is morning or night?
can she feel   me –
a train going through
my mountain,
my mother?

As if I moved   carriage three times
to be
forward-facing on the right-hand side,
sea-side

but the tide couldn't take the salt out of my
sweat
on that hospital bed of a train

The windows become mirrors,
too black to obscure
my face –
she never saw my face,
my mountain

Mountains don't bleed red you know,
they bleed dirty dishwater and sweat as their carriages are carried
away
to the drying rack

Nobody knows   loss   like my mountain –
the tide takes everything from her and its   reach
increases as the children on Downhill beach
wave

I look for her every time I ride the train
I only know her name,   'Binevenagh'
but she doesn't see my face or me,

the windows are black
and I can't see   out

TONY WALSH
POSH THINGS

Posh things:
Like in the catalogue and on the telly.
Like fridges and telephones.
Like visitors and watching BBC.

Posh things:
Like brown bread and plain milk.
Like strange fruit and vegetables.
Like tinned peaches and Battenburg cake.

Posh things:
Like Milk Tray and The Pop Man.
Like long matches and onyx ashtrays.
Like flowers and dentists.

Posh things:
Like football games and fairground rides.
Like banks and libraries.
Like holidays and trips to Stockport.

Posh things:
Like neat gardens and trained dogs.
Like spare rooms and spare change.
Like fitted carpets and soft towels.

Posh things:
Like... somewhere to go and... going there.
Like... wanting stuff and getting stuff.
Like... knowing stuff and... doing stuff.

Posh things; like paying for your school dinners. And leaving some.
Posh things; like new clothes and barber shops.
Posh things; like warm rooms and dry walls.
Posh things; like not lying and not needing to.
Posh things; like fucking confidence and That. Fucking. Look.

Posh things.
        Like fathers.
                And quietness.

All The Journeys
I Never Took

Rebecca Tantony

JENN HART
BETTER WATCH
YOUR MOUTH

JAM IS FOR GIRLS
GIRLS GET JAM

SHAGUFTA K IQBAL

EVERYTHING
WRONG
WITH
YOU
IS
BEAUTIFUL

TINA
SEDERHOLM

GOD SAVE
THE TEEN

ANDREW GRAVES

PERMEABLE

HANNAH CHUTZPAH

Requite

Malaika Kegode

TAKE
HAIR

ROB
AUTON

YOU SAD FEMINIST

MEGAN BEECH

In
The
Beginning
Was
The
Word

Daniel Cockrill
Damien Weighill

KATE FOX
CHRONOTOPIA

Through
your blood

Toby Campion

FERGUS
mcgonigal

EVERYONE
IS NOW
UNHAPPY

SHE GRRROWLS
THE ANTHOLOGY

We
Need
to
TALK

AGNES TÖRÖK

Deanna Rodger

SHRUTI CHAUHAN
RELATIONS

The first time I heard the words 'Uncle' and 'Aunt',
my face crumpled itself into a question mark.
Miss Pegg scoured the words onto the board
and on the floor, I shifted.
My hand shot up – she chose to ignore it.
"Miss?!" I implored, and instead of a
"Yes?" she brought a stern finger to her lip.
I groaned.
She didn't let me ask, what type of an
uncle? What type of an aunt?
Were they from my mother's side or my
father's? See, uncle, for me, was
crammed with obscurity and aunt, well, it felt
incomplete because I knew the truth! An aunt wasn't
an aunt, she was a *Kaki*, a *Masi*, a *Fuy* or a
Mami and an uncle wasn't an uncle, he was a *Masa*, a
Fua, a *Kaka*, or an *Ada*. Miss Pegg, I cried, this
aunt-uncle business is utter confusion
– confusion that is so easy to fix. A *Gujarati* suffix is all that is
needed: add *Kaka* to the back of a name, he's your
father's little brother, add *Masi* to a name, she's
the sister of your mother, and *Mami*, easy, she's
your mother's brother's wife and your father's
sister's husband is simply *Fua*! Like *Usha Kaki, Raj
Mama, Jayshree Masi, Amit Ada*.
Can't you see, Miss Pegg, it doesn't have
to be complicated! You just need to tidy this aunt-uncle
mess!

HANNAH CHUTZPAH
A DUDE IN AN EAST LONDON PUB HAS JUST OUT-JEWED ME

For Tim Wells

Judaism is an in-joke to me
A semi-secret identity
A smile when you find another
From your tribe.
'Oh, you were at that gig too?'
'Oh, you're a veggie too?'
'Oh, you're Jewish too?'

Yiddish is a breadcrumb trail I sprinkle
Into conversation
To see if anyone picks it up.

I am a half-Jewish, bisexual dual-national.
I live on a few fault lines
But I can blend right in
Or reveal my hand slightly
See if anyone picks up my clues:
Like more direct eye contact
Or gazing at another girl's lips.

Yiddish is my verbal garnish:
Adds so much texture
Couldn't cook a whole meal with it.

I leave breadcrumb trails
But tonight – four pints in –
I have drowned my subtlety.
Tonight I dropped a whole loaf of *challah* on the table:
'I liked your *frum* puns. I am Hannah Chutzpah.'

He shakes my hand
Replies in *three whole sentences* of Yiddish.
And a dude in an East London pub
Has just out-Jewed me
Just by speaking the language
I took my name from.

Helen Goldberg, Hinda Nisnievich
You would laugh if you could see me now
Your own great-granddaughter
Scrawling 'greenhorn' across her signature
In the Yiddish she cannot speak.

I dye my *shiksa* blonde hair darker
Am nostalgic for a New York I never knew
And wish for more links to the past
That you couldn't wait to escape.

Growing up second generation
Means growing grafted.
I flower in London soil.
The seam is small, the transplant took long ago
But the name I am happiest in
Is one I made up
Like you did at Ellis Island
Like my mother did in London.
Our tradition is transformation
…That, and shouting.

But I am a *shikkered shiksa* tonight
And a dude in an East London pub
Has just out-Jewed me
Just by speaking the language I do not speak
The language people use
To tell their kids to behave
To buy milk
To *kvetch*, to quip, to shout
In syntax, structure and sentences
In a language
– a whole language –
That I do not understand.

And my breadcrumbs are just breadcrumbs
A verbal garnish:
Adds so much texture
Couldn't cook a whole meal with it.

JAMAL MEHMOOD
WHAT IF THEY KNEW

nervous at the school gates
split fates and faces different
they ate rice with a fork
I with a spoon
my mother spoke her sweet punjabi
her sweet sweet punjabi
bended to every dialect
I stood by
itching to leave

what if they hear her
they'll remember I'm different
they'll ignore my face, won't they
they'll ignore her embroidery
they'll ignore her kameez
they'll ignore her shalwar
they'll ignore my name
while they say it so differently

mama and abu
clasping what they can
of what they left behind
those melodies and native tongue
on sunrise radio before school
I was itching to turn it down
close the door quickly
and turn my back on home

what if they heard where they come from
they'll ignore my ignorance
on pop culture references
they'll ignore my grandmother's broken english
sounding sweeter than a thousand sonnets in the queen's
if only I knew how sweet it was
I'd hold her hand a little tighter as she walked me home
where I'll always have to go
my grandfather scolds me in urdu
it burns twice
one for the scold
one for the urdu, one for the shame
I'm hoping he stops

they can't ignore that voice
what if they hear his journey
what if they hear the noble decision
what if they hear prison
what if they hear paris in the winter
what if they hear england spitting him out
what if they hear him swimming
what if they hear europe
what if they hear england saying come back
what if they hear him running

what if they hear the reason I'm here

SHAGUFTA K IQBAL
JAM IS FOR GIRLS, GIRLS GET JAM

But we awoke to the sizzle of eggs in the pan.
I like mine well done
and my sister liked hers with the yolk just so.
Yes, we were girls, yet we got eggs, not jam.

But. We were made to know:
I was not born boy,
I was not born to be man,
I was born to be given away
and that's why girls get jam.
And that is why I have not one
but three beautiful sisters.
Because I was not born boy.

And I was made to know that:
I escaped the desert sands,
my mouth was not placed over with hand.
I was lucky enough to be born after the gift of the Qur'an,
to be protected by the word of Allah.
And still my Ummah does not hear
the compassion bestowed upon us by Allah,
Still my Ummah chooses not to see
the light bestowed upon us by Allah.

Yes, bones lie scattered
criss-crossing through the deserts
under the feet of our beloved prophets.
And like my mother the desert heat suppresses secrets,
and mass graves gather under sand dunes.

No, I cannot tell you why that girl child,
buried breathing, lies in the embrace of the Sahara.

And yes, I must cover.
Live enshrouded.
Black cloth grazing against my skin,
protecting me from everyone else's sin.
My face, my eyes, my lips, my words and my honesty.
And yet I must pluck, and wax, and squeeze, and polish, and lipo,
and smile, full lips, big tits, designer vagina.
Because this way it gets called freedom.

You see, my identity and my honour lie not in me,
but in those who own me,
and oh, how they adorn me.
I tinsel like Christmas tree.
Purple bruises sparkle against my face.
Because in the land of the free,
by the man I love,
I am battered every fifteen seconds,
and in the land of democracy
I was only given the right to speak in 1918
'Shhhhhhhh, yes,' he said, 'hussssssssssssh,'
because only in 1991 did it become rape.
So 'Don't say a word,' he says.
But I, I've just got to ask, is that why even today
only 4.2% of rape cases lead to conviction in Bristol?
Yes, they all just let him walk away.

Because I was not born boy,
I was not born to be man.
I was born to be given away.
And that's why girls get jam.

And like traitors they say we give away land,
we do not carry on our fathers' names,
we disappear in family trees,
no one can trace who we are,
there is no leaf left for me.
And silent as sweltering nights,
we are considered to have come from thin air.
Giving birth to strong sons,
serving great husbands,
and burning to death on funeral pyres.
The Ganges just rolling on by,
unperturbed by that smell of burning flesh,
that stench of charred hair,
that one tumbled down a honey-brown back.

And they remind us
that we got lumbered with jam,
we were born to be given away
and no one loves those
who aren't here to stay.

VANESSA KISUULE
JJAJJA

I do not know you
I have composed you from
Dress cotton
Banana leaves
Patchwork quilts of quiet smiles and stories
That I could not understand
As I hold your hands
I know they've known more work in this past hour
Than mine will in their entire lifespan
I see the hardship of a thousand winds
Blowing across your face
So I trace a map of apologies
Across the fault lines of your fingers
And hope some amorphous ghost
Of my meaning lingers

You're a goddess
Your shoulder blades press together
Where your wings once met
And yet
We can only exchange
Awkward nods of acknowledgement
Because my world cannot slot into yours
Though I crawl on all fours
For meagre scraps of my identity
Endlessly grieving every mistranslation
Misunderstanding
Misinterpretation
Each seismic shift in time
I'm inventing you
Through a generation gone by
And as we sit in silence
Seedlings of the same wizened tree

I can imagine
I'd tell you of the short skirts girls in England wear
And the joys of Jeremy Kyle
How snow falls
Like capricious cotton balls of bliss
On nights cold as an Eskimo's kiss
I'd ask of the past

The laughter shared
The songs once sung
What Mum was like when she was young
If I weren't trapped with the handicap
Of my British tongue

I envision the talks we'd have
Tucked in the candlelit cave of a power cut
Cradled in a clash of culture
Hoping the Tower of Babel might bleed into oblivion
And somehow
A tainted miracle might unfurl
I'm willing to bet
We'd have been the best of friends
In a different world
But I do not know you
I've composed you from
Dress cotton
Banana leaves
Patchwork quilts of quiet smiles and stories
That I could not understand
In this land of lost language
I am neither stranger nor native
The weight of my wasted words
Cannot be translated

*Jjajja: Luganda for 'Grandmother'

MICHELLE MADSEN
LITTLE GREEN MEN

Astrophysicist Jocelyn Bell Burnell discovered pulsars (pulsating stars) in 1967 while a postgraduate student at Cambridge. Her thesis supervisor Anthony Hewish won the Nobel Prize for Physics for the discovery in 1974 alongside radio astronomer Martin Ryle. Bell Burnell was overlooked by the prize-giving committee despite being responsible for the discovery, one of the most notable of the 20th century.

A thick halo of light rings your eye.
Child's lashes flicker in the morning sun
Lay flat against a waxen eyelid
As you fight the urge to blink

Curious, if unimpressed by syllabuses and classroom chat
Your brain skirts the universe in bold leaps
Set free by a visit to the observatory
Icarus would have envied your wings.

A blink, a pulsing flash of time
And you're beating back the Glasgow rain,
In classes with girls who listen and answer
But knit booties for future babies under their books
Men don't like girls who are too clever, they say.

But you're watching the shutter slide back
Over the telescope's voyaging eye
Feeling your heart jump as it's pushed to the lens
The havoc the stars play on its strings

This is it, life beyond imagination
Kiss the sky, eat it up

By the banks of the Cam the ground shifts
Opens a door to another world
As the people come and go
Trickling stream and careless laughter

You, eyes to the sky,
Grow strong, sinews tighten and tan
From clinging to tops of telegraph poles.
This week you'll map the universe

Listening in to other worlds
As Phoebus heaves the earth ever forward
And when the science men,
Nodding and wise in their Scandinavian towers,
Forget that it was you
Ear pressed to the door of life
Who heard the blips
The dancing feet of little green men
The warning lighthouse flares
Of a thousand ghosts of suns
Re-writing our understanding of life,
You'll ruffle your child's hair,
Climb the telescope, eyes tipped to the sky,
Lid rimmed in a halo, unearthly bright,
And smile.

DEANNA RODGER
HOW TO BE A FEMINIST

Want what I haven't got.

Wear what I want.
Short skirts.
Low tops.
High heels.
(Fuck the twat that said not to wear high heels so the creepy shadow
man can't hear me, they are a weapon and if my knees and hips
weren't so bad I would wear them more often because high heels are
boom and it's mainly because of the walk and
click they make.)

Love women
who own their bodies and their rights and their homes and their
cars and their bus pass.

Let armpit hair grow free.
Shave and wax and epilate when the friction becomes an irritant.

Paint nails.
Don't hide the chip.

Wear deodorant but don't look like I do.
Be invisible.

Don't be invisible.
Hate women
when they decide they don't agree with me.

Hate myself.

When nobody notices me,
love my sexy body.
Have sex.
Don't apologise.
Be 'free'.

Sleep with boyfriends, male friends, friends of friends, cheaters and
foreigners, liars and dealers, drummers and rappers, players and
professionals.
Don't feel like a whore.
Get drunk and fuck everyone
at the same time

in a tent.
Wake up and

leave them – before breakfast if possible.
If not,

don't wash the dishes.
Never wash the dishes
until there are no more dishes.
Love men

who carry bags
and pay for things
and go down
and cook
and listen
and agree.
Hate dicks

when they decide they don't want to be with us
and their mouths turn into giant arseholes that want to suck our matter
in to fart their gas out.

Fart, belch, don't giggle, stern face,
subtweet and avoid confrontation, bitch.
Don't use the word *bitch* unless chanting a hip-hop song.
Don't let anyone use the word *bitch* unless quoting a male
rapper.
Call Beyoncé and Rihanna my bitches 'cause they obviously
don't mind.
Become a role model.
Be a feminist.

Never stop changing.
Don't forget.
Let go.
Forgive.
Expect whistles and slow cars,
accept but don't slow for them.
Boast in conversations
over every sound.
Think before you speak.
Create judgement.
Answer.
Retweet.

Form an army of followers.
Unfollow unfollowers.
Lead.
Be strong.
Be happy.
Be thin.
Run.
Date,
and be grateful.
Don't piss on the seat.
Don't sit on the seat.
Wipe the piss off the seat.
Hate 'Shewees' – stand for squatting.
Demand safe night toilets for women.
Don't be embarrassed by your tampon.
Pay for your period.
Buy stress.
Follow trends.
Try 'Shewees' – hate street lights.
Laugh loudly and shout, fall over other women.
Scrabble to stand tall.
Be opinionated.
Form an opinion.
Buy it with the second round of rosé and sambuca shots.
Be intelligent, witty, pretty, sharp, judgemental, blunt.
Possess an opinion.
Get noticed through it.
Throw it up like regurgitated 3am chips on a bus, falling out of a sexy
dress and high heels.
@everyone
#Gethomesafe.
It's your right, to get home safe.
Write it
but don't read the comments.

Never read the comments.

MAIRI CAMPBELL-JACK
NARCISSUS HAD A WIFE YOU KNOW…

she would arrange his hair
while he gazed, clipping it
to perfectly frame his face
as his looking deepens his love.

She would drape his cloak
on him when it was cold,
at times pointing out features
he may have missed in his contemplation.

One day, catching her own reflection
she noticed a sagging round her jaw,
a line by her eyes. Looking down she saw
her hands, in his cloak, looked more like her mother's.

After that his hair grew,
and threatened to cover his eyes.

LYDIA TOWSEY
INTERVIEW WITH A BARBIE

Do you ever get tired of smiling?
In the street do passers-by say –
A: Frown!
B: But, Barbie – you're
anatomically incapable of walking.
Your torso's far too small to hold in all your organs.
You should be moving on fours, given your proportions.
Your waist's the same circumference as your head! Or –
C: Barbie, do you plan to kill again?

Did you ever wonder why you couldn't age?
Or why your heels were all so high?
Or why, though your favourite food is burgers
and you love to bake,
you never seem to eat
or put on any weight?
Barbie, is that murder in your eyes...

or are you just thinking about Ken?
And – how is the sex?
I wouldn't want to pry
but the lack of any bits
makes me think that you must
do it in some – special way?

Did you ever consider a
career in academia
but note the lack
of an accessorising attaché case?

And that there are few Football Barbies,
Army Barbies, Banker Barbies

or Barbies working on the stock exchange –
but you can be a (Class) President Barbie, or
Veterinary Surgeon Barbie –
as long as you keep it pink.
Or Mermaid Barbie. Or grow a pair
of wings...

Barbie, is that murder in your eyes
or are you checking in? Barbie –
have you ever considered

(more) plastic surgery
and wished (if only)
there was an online
child-friendly app to help?

Are you thinking about Ken?
Are you thinking about hairstyles?

Barbie... is that a head in your handbag?
A leg – jutting out the fridge?
Are you thinking about pets?
Are you thinking about travel?

Is that blood on the curtain?
In the shower? In the Dreamhouse?
In the Barbie Mariposa Princess Fairy Castle
on the butterfly-accented bedstead
and balconette and chandelier,
sprayed on the canopy,
the dressing table,
mirror set,
the limited

edition wallpaper
and ball-gowns
and twinsets
and rollers
and lipstick
accessories...
Running.
Pooling.
Splattered.
Barbie? ...Barbie?

...Babs?
!

MALAIKA KEGODE
OWL & PUSSYCAT

There are air bubbles under your skin
like dried wallpaper. All self-absorbed, self-serving
puncture wounds, gnat-bite redness.
I ask again why you do this.

Is it still to follow in the footsteps of those
sad-eyed musicians you always admired,
whose early graves only added poignancy to the
beauty-scarred lyrics that danced around your head
at fourteen?
Practice rolling joints with shaky hands in your room,
hoping your mum wouldn't walk in to see your chrysalis shedding
to reveal the mirror image of her ex-lover, same one
whose hands formed into claws and legs bent backwards
in chase of that sticky black tar smack.

I tried to stop writing about you.
But four years is a long time to lose your mind, and now I've checked
out early. Tried to steady the beat of my heart so that I can wake
up now before noon, look at the moon with someone
other than you, still feel its beauty.

Too long had we been marooned by the promise of
white rum midnights, honey, money: rolled-up five pound notes.
And we tried to stop each other from drowning not knowing
the ocean was growing because of our salty tears, my dear,
we were always shipwrecked.
Our own worst enemy.

But don't get me wrong, I still remember nights in front of my
too-small TV. Always full of pizza and beer, my dear,
please don't think I've forgotten.

But a few good nights does not amend cruelty,
as you were to me when I was no help to your recovery.

If I have learnt anything from this little life that we have shared
it's that people aren't there to be saved,
and to try this only causes hurricanes.
Love should not be founded in pain.

Every hope of mine is in you, but I have checked out early.
I'm going to bed early with a cup of green tea
and I smile now, widely.

Love has slipped through my fingers.

Every hope of mine is in you,
this I know you know.
But this is my one last, final sigh
of letting go.

REBECCA TANTONY
BAKED APRICOTS

I found Allah once.
It was Morocco seven years ago,
my knees collapsed on a prayer mat,
arms flat-packed behind my back,
heart beating like that of a racehorse.
It was thirty-four degrees of hot sun.
Baked apricots, speakers spitting prayers.
Me looking everywhere for God.
Awkward and still, waiting for
the return of my breath.
When suddenly I saw him.
Old now, ninety or so,
bending down and picking up fag butts
and somehow I then knew
he too was trying to bring back
that which you just need to give up.

I found the Guru once.
Outside a gurdwara in Bristol.
She was a woman waiting
in a short skirt and high heels,
four children pulling on every limb,
her still smiling somehow.
It was a dry day
and she spoke to them all
as if she were speaking in scriptures,
promised pack lunches and trips to the parks.
Kindness revealing itself as miracles –
tapping Morse codes across her children's skin,
saying, 'Let me in through every single pore of you.'

I found God once.
Aged nine, St Francis Church, sat between
Emilie Slade and Kimberly Chapman.
It was the assembly first thing; all clapping hands,
we sang old forgotten hymns of birth and stars.
Instead, I looked out the window,
watched wind pass through tree leaves.
Watched the sun spread the sky red,
an ink blot on tracing paper.
Watched nature move together perfectly.

*

Don't just find me on Sundays,
somewhere pious, somewhere forgotten,
quietly timetabling God's entrance.
Turn me into a hymn,
for I will never know silence like I do now.
Playing songs across your gravestone, God,
trying to wake the life out of your peace,
I spent too much time editing
your face out of the black days,
scratching the surface of my heart.

I always thought you were a fairy tale,
a man-made cut-out, a ridiculous promise
that never came true.
But I've seen through you now;
you're standing in the newsagent's,
in the shopkeepers and customers.
In the bus drivers and check-out girls.
In the debt collectors, babysitters
and dinner ladies. You're in the waitress
and the bartender, in my mother's
phone calls. I'm sure you were there too, God,
when I never called my father back.
When I thought the plane would crash.
When I swam out of my depth
and nearly drowned.

I'm sorry I didn't find you before.
I found my expectancy.
I'll rest next to you now, fall asleep and dream
of electricity bringing us back together.
I'll dream of discovering you
in my own tangible way,
amongst my own tangible people.

I'll dream of looking for the sacred
and finding holy in everyone.

CHRIS REDMOND
LET THE PIG OUT

Eddie is twelve years old and timid.
I'm teaching him the drums
but there's something lacking.

I say, Eddie,
your hi-hats are steady,
snare's rocking the two and four,
bass drum's pushing off beats.
It's red raw,
but you've got meat on the bone now.
But Eddie, tell me what you're drumming for,
because these beats are not fat-back.
They're not even a wet slap.
You can't cook at this temperature.

It's said a drummer can summon spirits
from Africa's pulsing core, whose voices
have been echoing through every generation
since our ancestors first stood on two feet.
But right now you're pushing this beat around
like food on a plate you haven't had to work for.
Like a too-polite, under the breath, apologetic,
ever so, thank you, please, could I?
Should I? Play it… like… this?

Eddie, whoever's holding you down,
I'm taking their foot off your neck,
so look up.
Untether yourself.
We need to make libations to the drum gods.
Drink, I'll summon them.
We need to light a fire here,
wrap ourselves in smoke. Remember,
this is wood in your hands
and the polymer you strike
still holds the moniker of skin.
Not long ago, calves died
for you to play beats on their hide,
so at least do them the honour
of playing with a passion
befitting of such a sacrifice.

Eddie. Let the pig out.

Eddie says, 'What do you mean?'

Let the pig out.
There's no other way to say it.
Let the pig out.
It's all about how you play
this grunty, funky,
heavy-arsed, munchy,
angry stink of a
muddy-guts, pink or
white or black with a
hairy fat belly. Let the
pig out, Eddie, let the
beats get smelly.
Let the pig out.

Let the hi-hats splash,
get the snare drum cracking.
Push the beat across the bar,
then kick the fucker back in.
Let the pig out.

That pig is Gullinbursti,
steed of Norse god Freyr,
who spreads light through the land
with his golden hair.
That pig pulls Marici,
Buddhist goddess of the heavens,
all-seeing, holding the sun
and moon in her hands.
That pig belongs to Set,
brother and enemy of Osiris.
Set becomes the god
of chaos and darkness.
That pig is Varaha,
incarnation of Vishnu,
who fought and won a thousand-year
battle to save the Earth, Eddie,
and it's you, c'mon,
the pig is inside.
And when you release the beast,
cast your worries to one side.
It'll untie your tongue-tie,

trample your burden.
The pig is your friend, Eddie.
Of that much I'm certain.
Let the pig out.

To the kid getting bullied at school
'cause he's different. Let the pig out.

To the girl with a song in her heart
but no one to sing to. Let the pig out.

To every artist, writer, dancer,
poet, musician. Let the pig out.

To the people around the world
standing up for change. Let the pig out.

To the nurse who lost her job
so the banker can keep his bonus. Let the pig out.

To the widow who learns beyond grief,
there's a choice. Let the pig out.

To the bipolar explorer choosing
adventure and medication. Let the pig out.

To every little Eddie,
finding a voice.

PETE BEARDER
RUNNING OUT OF PAPER

Cordoned off in the reading corner
me and my best friend Eddie sat
facing books. But when the teacher
was out of sight, he'd jump
forty pages, then pretend to keep on reading.

Eddie was a Coke can shaken and left.
He always wanted to be somewhere else.
He'd swear words and insults
about his stepmum and dad
scratched all over his walls.

What he lacked in the field of study he made up
in the field of sport and talk;
he never fitted in the A4 margins
but when he had a football and a point to make
Eddie spelled well with his feet.

The last time I saw him was after expulsion,
alone in the school yard with a score to settle.
Miss Smyth told us all to get away from the window.
We shuddered as he wrote Fuck You on the glass.

HENRY RABY
SUPERMAN IS A REFUGEE

I have the power.

As a teenager, my main priority with adolescent evolution
was an attempt to develop super human abilities.

I used to try and stick to my bedroom wall, hold out my hand to
summon energy bolts or try and move things with my mind.

It did not take long to establish I had not developed mutant powers

At school, I would imagine what it would be like if Oaklands
Secondary School was Hogwarts, with the majority of students sorted
into Nobhead House.

Assuming my genetics just gave me bad acne, a funny walk and the
inability to grow a proper beard, I settled on waiting for an irradiated
animal, cosmic ray or gamma radiation, because obviously they're all
safe, right?

So far, I'm still waiting.

I waited for an elderly man to come and reveal my place in a master
plan involving light sabres, magic rings or sword in the stones
because obviously I must be important, right?

I'm still waiting.

But I have a power with language. Wherever I go in the world my
English tongue will be enough.

When I travel, customs will never suspect I am secretly a would be
world-conquering mastermind, despite most super-villains, like super-
heroes, being white men.

In books, television, films, I see myself. In the history books, the
characters on television, the crew of films. The law-makers. I see
myself.

No one has ever mistaken me for a bird, or a plane.

For the record, I've always got onto planes willingly.

But the ghost of Jimmy Mubenga doesn't need wings

I suspect everyone has a secret identity. I suspect the reason phone boxes still exist is we all need to take a moment to shelter in a private space as we prepare ourselves for the outside world full of buildings we can't leap over, locomotives more powerful than us and bullets we can't outrun.

For the record, I've never had to outrun a bullet.

But the ghost of Jean Charles de Menezes is outpacing Tube trains

I am not a shape-shifter, and no one will ever confuse, or challenge, my gender. I will probably never be the object of a song. I will probably never be the object of a joke. I will probably never be the subject for an insulting Channel 4 documentary. My Big Fat Nerd Punk Poet Wedding.

I pray the ghost of Vicky Thompson doesn't haunt her all-male prison. Superman is a refugee, escaping destruction and seeking sanctuary. It's just a lucky coincidence he's from the western side of Krypton.

Even if Batman's parents weren't murdered, he'd still be using his wealth to hurt people with mental illnesses.

And this may not be a super-power, but it is the power of privilege.

My career aspirations were, and still are: pirate, ninja and/or dinosaur. But if I was pumped full of chemicals at the behest of my government to fight for truth and justice as a super-soldier, I would petition my commanding officer to grant me the freedom not to wear my country's flag on my costume, sorry, uniform.

The flag of my country appears on my passport, the default setting for languages, hoodys, key rings, pencil sharpeners, teddy bears, border control uniforms, bombs and the drones which drop them.

SCOTT TYRRELL
IF WE'RE BEING HONEST

If we're being honest
I'm broken in the places I didn't expect
strong in places I rarely visit
more thorough than my cavalier demeanor
would have you believe
and more wounded by
being ignored than insulted

If we're being honest
I eat more ice cream whilst spooning it into the bowl
than what actually goes into the bowl
I pee in the shower
find pooing strangely erotic
and throw my clipped toenails behind the telly
If we're being honest
I drink more than I used to
run less than I used to
weigh more than I used to
and masturbate at a consistent level
and sometimes when pets can see me or if I can
hear the voice of my child in the other room

If we're being honest
I respect cats more than dogs
because cats tend to leave the room
If they see me masturbating

If we're being honest
I don't like much poetry
because some of it is tedious
thinly-veiled self-aggrandizement
and some of it is better than
my ignorance can tell
and reading mine often reveals
all too painfully which camp it belongs
which, if the former,
I pretend overlaps with the latter

And if we're being really honest
some of it isn't actually poetry
but I'm hoping you won't be able to tell

If we're being honest
putting spoken word
in a book makes as much sense
as buying a printed screenplay
or listening to a tour
of an art gallery on the radio

If we're being honest
things aren't always political
and sometimes people just want to
get through the day without joining
any dots
If we're being honest
the left is far more cunning at
truth selection than the right
because we care deeply about
the right not being right

If we're being honest
most monsters are just people
stuck in a temporary swamp
not strong enough yet to take
the hand more people
should be holding out

If we're being honest
I hated my mother for twenty years
until I saw her be a grandmother
then I hated myself for not seeing
the wood of grace and patience
for the tree of resentment

If we're being honest
I'm not honest enough to be fully honest
because the accidental cup of lies
I spilled on the mountain top of youth
is now an immovable glacier in the valley of middle-age

If we're being honest
I'm shit at metaphors

If we're being honest
most religion doesn't hurt despite its dishonesty
and atheism doesn't hurt those who prefer dishonesty
and passive aggressiveness isn't charming

If we're being honest
In truth or dare I'll always tell the truth
because the truth behind me is easier to cope with
than the coercion in front

If we're being honest
the phrase 'if we're being honest'
Is a brutal preamble
the cliff before the tempest
the creaking door opening on a winter's night
the harsh light on the operating table
the slow sit down with hands clasped

If we're being honest
invokes a cold intake of breath
because if we're being honest
It precedes words we can rarely take back
But If we're being honest
we shouldn't need to.

More information on all our poets and
books can be found
by visiting:

burningeye.bigcartel.com